CliffsNotes®

Roadmap
to
College

CliffsNotes®

Roadmap to College

Navigating Your Way to
College Admission Success

by Karen Wolf, M.S.

WILEY

Wiley Publishing, Inc.

For general information on our other products and services or to obtain technical support please contact our Customer Care Department within the U.S. at (877) 762-2974, outside the U.S. at (317) 572-3993 or fax (317) 572-4002.

Wiley also publishes its books in a variety of electronic formats. Some content that appears in print may not be available in electronic books. For more information about Wiley products, please visit our web site at www.wiley.com.

Library of Congress Cataloging-in-Publication Data

Wolf, Karen, 1958-
  CliffsNotes roadmap to college : navigating your way to college admission success / by Karen Wolf.
     p. cm.
  ISBN-13: 978-0-470-47442-6
  ISBN-10: 0-470-47442-4
  1. College preparation programs--United States. 2. Universities and colleges--United States--Admission. I. Title. II. Title: Cliffs notes roadmap to college.
  LB2351.2.W649 2009
  378.1'61--dc22
                              2009034017
Printed in the United States of America

10 9 8 7 6 5 4 3 2 1

Book production by Wiley Publishing, Inc., Composition Services

I would like to dedicate CliffsNotes Roadmap to College *to my mother, Hanna Jawetz and to my late father, Eric Jawetz, for their inspiration, love, and support.*

Acknowledgments

I want to thank the dedicated and professional staff at Wiley Publishing, Inc. for their guidance and support, especially Senior Editor Greg Tubach and Project Editor Suzanne Snyder. Special gratitude to Grace Freedson, my literary agent, for bringing me this wonderful opportunity.

I am deeply indebted to the college admissions officers who contributed their collective years of wisdom and advice to students throughout the book. These dedicated professionals are:

- Cheryl Brown, Director of Undergraduate Admissions, Binghamton University, State University of New York
- Lauren A. Kay, Assistant Director, Indiana University–Bloomington
- Raymond Lutzky, Director of Outreach, Rensselaer Polytechnic Institute, Troy, New York
- Nancy J. Maly, Director of Admission, Grinnell College, Grinnell, Iowa
- Paul Marthers, EdD, Dean of Admission, Reed College, Portland, Oregon
- Joan Isaac Mohr, Vice President and Dean of Admissions, Quinnipiac University, Hamden, Connecticut
- Jacquelyn Nealon, EdD, Vice President of Enrollment Services, New York Institute of Technology, Old Westbury, New York
- Lorne Robinson, Dean of Admissions and Financial Aid, Macalester College, St. Paul, Minnesota
- Mitchell L. Thompson, Jr., Dean of Students, Scarsdale High School, Scarsdale, New York and former Associate Dean of Admission and Records, The Cooper Union, New York, New York
- Dominic Yoia, Senior Director of Financial Aid, Quinnipiac University, Connecticut

Special appreciation to Rafi Abrahams, Michael Heino, Ben Kaye, and Kayla Reinstein, who contributed their beautiful essays to this project; much success to each of you on your bright futures.

A special thank you to Joan Parmet for being an inspiring role model to me, and for taking me under her wing and imparting her wisdom. I enjoy working with Joan as well as my valued colleagues and friends Arlette Miller and Susan Szaluta. Thank you to the administrators, staff, and students at HAFTR HS; it has become my second home. Thank you to NACAC, the professional association which provides counselors, students, and parents with many resources to use during the college admissions process.

Finally, I want to thank my husband Jonathan, and my daughters Marissa and Ilana. I appreciate your love, patience and understanding during this project when my time and attention was limited. A special thank you to Ilana, who was my research assistant; your help was invaluable.

Table of Contents

About the Author

Karen Wolf is a college guidance counselor at the Hebrew Academy of Five Towns and Rock-away (HAFTR) High School, a private high school in Cedarhurst, New York. She is a certified School Counselor, having received her M.S. in Education from Hofstra University. She has a second master's degree in Industrial/Organizational Psychology from Rensselaer Polytechnic Institute. She has a B.A. in Psychology with an adjunct in Management from Binghamton University, State University of New York. Before becoming a college guidance counselor, Karen held several positions in the public and private sectors as a management consultant and a training-and-development/organization-development professional.

Introduction

❝Congratulations! I am thrilled to inform you that you have been admitted to our university's freshman class entering fall 2009. You can be proud of your achievements and I am confident that you will contribute to the long-standing tradition of excellence that has characterized our students.❞

—Excerpt from an acceptance letter
from a large Midwest public university

Hopefully, at the end of the college admissions process, you will receive a similar letter and you will join the ranks of college graduates. College is a place where you grow academically, psychologically, and socially. You will also gain financially as completing a four year college degree has a financial impact as well. According to the Census Bureau, high school graduates are expected to earn about $1.2 million over their lifetime, students completing some college will earn about $1.5 million and college graduates will earn about $2.1 million. The value of a college education is much more than financial; its value is priceless.

There are several important trends in the college admissions process about which you should be aware. There are shifting demographics in the numbers and types of students applying to college. According to a report by the National Association of College Admissions Counselors (NACAC), a professional association consisting of college admissions officers, guidance counselors and private consultants, the overall number of high school graduates will slowly decline after fifteen years of increases. Some parts of the country, however, will see increases in high school graduating classes such as states in the South and Southwest. There is a growing minority population as well as a lopsided shift in the number of males versus females attending college. The gender gap in college students has been reported nationally as approximately 60% female to 40% male. In some colleges, the ratio is as high as 70% female versus 30% male. In other colleges, the ratio has been purposely balanced at 50% male and 50% female, while in technically oriented institutions the ratio could be reversed with higher percentages of male students. All of these trends may result in changes in the recruitment strategies that colleges use to attract students, thereby impacting college admissions.

Another trend that impacts you and your family is the spiraling cost of a college education. According to the National Trust, a non-profit educational think tank, there has been a 150%–200% increase in the cost of attending college over the last 25 years. What also increases the price of a college education is the number of students who actually graduate in four years. Unfortunately, the norm is for students *not* to complete college in four years, as evidenced by the way many colleges report their graduation statistics in terms of the number of students graduating in *six* years. Part of the reason why students take more than four years to complete college is that they are not adequately prepared for the rigors of college, they do not always carefully research potential colleges, and many students change their major several times during their college career. These factors also affect the transfer rate, which is estimated to be about 20%. Carefully selecting a college (Chapter 10), doing a self assessment (Chapter 2), and choosing a college which offers several potential majors in which you are interested can positively impact how long it takes to finish college.

Still another critical aspect facing college applicants today is the testing frenzy that has become a dominant factor in college admissions over the last ten years or so. There is a growing dissatisfaction in the guidance counselor community and the larger community about the priority placed on standardized tests (SAT and ACT). As a result of this concern over testing, there is a growing trend towards "testing optional" schools as well as a potential re-evaluation of the usefulness and significance of these tests. For now though, testing remains a vital component of the college admissions process.

ROADMAP TO COLLEGE

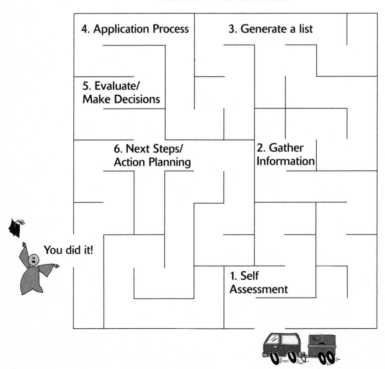

In light of all of the factors discussed so far, how does one find the "right college"? Should you look for the most selective college you can get into? Should you spend the big bucks on undergraduate school or should you focus on getting a solid, quality education at a reasonable price and go for a "name brand" school for graduate school? Are these things mutually exclusive? Should you go to your "dream school?" Is there an "only one school for you" approach to choosing a college? These are philosophical questions for which there are no easy answers. I have met parents who firmly believe that their child should obtain a liberal arts education at a city or state university and then attend a super selective (and usually more expensive) school for graduate school. Then there are parents who want their child to attend a prestigious undergraduate college as they believe their child will then have a better chance of attending a top graduate school.

The search for the right colleges for you can be daunting and quite stressful. Most students are 17–18 years of age when they are making one of the most important decisions of their lives. Parents can add to that stress by either pushing their children too hard or conversely by not taking enough of an interest in the college search. Then there is peer pressure, where many students feel pressured into applying to the same schools as their friends and they are afraid to go their own way even if it is in their best interest to do so. How does one deal with all of this stress during the last one to two years of high school? By having honest and open conversations with your parents, friends, and relatives some of the stress can be reduced. Asking for help from your guidance counselor and others is another way to minimize stress. Getting to know your guidance counselor early in your high school career is a smart idea, even if it's just to see them a few times a year for a brief visit or to say hello. Planning ahead, abiding by deadlines, and doing careful research can also alleviate some of the anxiety. Remember who the most important person in this process is—you.

Self-Assessment

I love the patterns and complexities of numbers.

I love painting and drawing people and objects.

I love writing stories and analyzing literature.

I love building things and I love the physics of rollercoasters.

I like helping people with their problems.

How would you describe yourself? Are you creative, a problem solver, an analytical person, a planner, a motivator, a teacher? Where do you see yourself in 5, 10, or even 20 years? How do your family and friends describe your personality? Before you even consider applying to college, it's worthwhile to take a step back and take a good look at yourself.

What are my strengths and weaknesses?

Do you excel in math, science, art, music, social science, or humanities courses? By learning more about yourself, your interests, and your preferences, you will be able to make a more informed decision about which colleges best meet your needs.

Some high schools require that you formalize a self-assessment by taking a career or interest inventory before meeting with a guidance counselor, usually in your junior year, to discuss prospective colleges. Most of these inventories evaluate your personality style and assess your preference (not whether or not you'll be successful) for different types of careers. Many of these assessments are based on the works of psychologist Carl Jung and the mother-daughter team of Katharine Briggs and Isabel Briggs Myers, developers of the Myers Briggs Type Indicator (MBTI).

Some states offer students free services, which combine self-assessment tools with college and career searches, along with opportunities to develop a resume. For example, the New York and California Web sites have links to "The Interest Profiler," a 20–30 minute online personality assessment tool with potential career matches. The federal government also offers many resources that allow you to explore potential careers, obtain salary information, and identify jobs in high demand in the future. One very useful Web site is www.online.onetcenter.org, which offers detailed career information that is linked to the Bureau of Labor Statistics. Another useful Web site, www.dwya.com, is based on the very popular career book, *Do What You Are* (Little, Brown & Co., 2001), and is a great resource for determining your personality type.

Checklist for taking inventory

Students sometimes take interest inventories and say, "Oh, it didn't work for me; the test said I was going to be a bank teller or a hairdresser." What these instruments do is assess your preferences (not strengths) in dealing with people, processing information, making decisions, and organizing your life. They are not foolproof, but they are useful in gaining data about yourself. The checklist below can be used to highlight your strengths and areas for improvement. Getting to know who you are will assist you in writing essays and forming a list of potential colleges.

In the checklist below, use a ✔ to indicate your agreement.

Self-Assessment: Taking Inventory			
Area of Assessment:	*Agree*	*Unsure*	*Disagree*
PERSONALITY			
I describe myself as an extrovert (I prefer to be around people; I don't mind large crowds; I am outer-directed).			
I describe myself as an introvert (I prefer to be alone; I am quiet and inner-directed).			
I prefer to process information through the use of my five senses; I am detail oriented; I like facts and figures.			
I prefer to process information through my intuition; I look for the big picture; I am an "ideas" person.			
I prefer to make decisions based on logic and rational thinking; justice and fairness are important to me.			
I prefer to make decisions based on my feelings and how decisions will affect people.			
I prefer to plan activities ahead of time; I am decisive and I like to finish projects that I start.			
I prefer to be spontaneous; I am flexible and don't always finish tasks but I like to start many projects.			

Area of Assessment:	Agree	Unsure	Disagree
ACADEMIC HISTORY			
I am an above-average student.			
I am an average student.			
I am a below-average student.			
My grades are consistent.			
I have challenged myself with honors, Advanced Placement (AP), or International Baccalaureate (IB) courses.			
I am an active participant in the classroom.			
I have worked hard and tried to improve my grades.			
EXTRACURRICULAR ACTIVITIES			
I am very involved in school clubs and out-of-school activities.			
I perform community service.			
I have held a part-time or full-time job.			
I have had an unpaid or paid internship.			
I have had challenging summer experiences.			
TALENTS/ABILITIES			
I have a special talent (art, music, singing, and writing).			
I play a sport.			
I would like to play a sport competitively.			
I have a learning disability and require support services.			
I have good writing skills.			
I can communicate well verbally.			
COLLEGE PREFERENCES			
I would like to commute to college.			
I would like to live in a dorm room at college.			
I would like to attend a college within a 2-hour drive from home.			

continued

Area of Assessment:	Agree	Unsure	Disagree
I would like to attend a college within a 4-hour drive from home.			
I would like to attend a college more than 4 hours away from home.			
I am not opposed to taking a plane ride to and from college.			
I prefer a city environment.			
I prefer a suburban campus environment.			
I prefer a rural campus environment.			
I want to attend a same-sex college.			
I want to attend a parochial college.			
I want to attend a diverse campus.			
I want to attend a Historically Black college.			
The cost of my college education is a major concern.			
I want to attend a small university (2,500 students or less).			
I want to attend a medium university (8,000 students or less).			
I want to attend a large university (20,000 students or less).			
I want to attend a super-sized university (more than 20,000 students).			

What are my family's values and desires?

What your parents and other family members think can greatly influence your choice of college. Some parents prefer that their children follow in their path and attend the college where they went. This option is referred to in admissions jargon as a *legacy admission,* and in some selective institutions legacy admits are given preference in the admissions process, especially if their parents have given substantial amounts of money. Other parents want their children to follow their own path and have opportunities that they didn't have. Parents who attended a commuter college may want their child to have the "full college experience" as an on-campus student.

There may also be financial and family constraints, which will dictate where you will go to college. It is important to discuss financial, geographical, and family-related (divorce, illness) issues up front so you know what your options are during the college search process. I know of students who applied to and were accepted to the college of their dreams, only to be told later that they couldn't attend that college because their parents couldn't afford it or because they needed to be closer to home for family reasons. It's important to have an honest and open discussion early on about factors which could take certain colleges out of the picture to avoid miscommunication and disappointment. Taking into account the wishes and desires of families is a key element of the college search process.

Should I choose a major on the application?

Every college application asks you to "select a potential major" or to indicate an "area of concentration." How should you answer this question? The answer depends on the individual. Approximately 50 percent of students applying to college answer that they are an "undecided major," because they really have no idea what career path to choose and they don't have a particular strength in one area, such as science. The other 50 percent of students have been able to focus on a particular area in high school. They may know people (especially parents, family members, or friends) in a certain field or they may have had a part-time job or an internship and have been able to narrow the list down to a field of study, such as business, and even more specifically, accounting. Others may have taken a career assessment, which indicates the types of job categories in which they would prefer to work. If you are in the group where you do have an area of interest, then there could be an advantage in applying to a particular major in a university.

> **TIP:** I know two students who applied to a large public university. One applied as an "undecided" major and the other student applied as a math major. Their grades and standardized test scores were similar, but the student who listed math as her major was accepted, whereas the other student was not accepted. This example may be extreme, but it could happen.

The major you have selected could be an "under-represented" major, where there is a low volume of students and therefore a college may accept more students into this major. Also, sometimes colleges add new programs of study or they hire new faculty members to expand an existing major. If they are looking to accept students into this major and you can demonstrate an interest in these areas, you may have a slight advantage in being accepted.

The best advice is to be true to yourself and to remember that even if you do select a major, in most cases you can change your major when you arrive on campus or later on. Most colleges don't require you to select a major until at least the second semester of your sophomore year. It is likely though that you will be assigned an academic advisor in the field that you designate as your major. My daughter applied to college as an anthropology major, and she has had the same advisor since freshman year. She has been able to forge a strong bond with him, which is a definite advantage.

Applying with a Stated Major versus an Undecided Major: Views from Our Admissions Counselors' Panel

"A stated major is regarded only as a statement of preliminary interest. Being undecided is not a problem at all; at Grinnell, exploring new possibilities is expected. Interest in a major not offered raises questions about any potential match with the College and the applicant's understanding of the College."–Nancy J. Maly, Director of Admissions, Grinnell College

"Rensselaer operates 'low walls' between our academic units, and does not employ different admissions criteria among majors. Anyone who is admitted to Rensselaer is admitted, regardless of major, and can switch majors with ease. Ultimately, if a student is not sure which major they want, they should apply 'undeclared' and allow Rensselaer's Advising and Learning Assistance Center to help them select a major once they have arrived." –Raymond Lutzky, Director of Outreach, Rensselaer Polytechnic Institute

"Some students apply to Binghamton knowing what they want to major in. We encourage those students to apply to the appropriate professional school (i.e., engineering, nursing, business) because each has specific admissions requirements. However, some of our students do not apply to Binghamton with a stated major. That's perfectly fine. After all, college is the chance to explore different studies, career paths and professional and personal interests."–Cheryl Brown, Director of Admission, Binghamton University, State University of New York

"Every student is viewed based on the same standards, regardless of major. It doesn't help or hinder a student to declare a major. If a student isn't sure what he/she wants to major in, we offer 'exploratory' as an option on the application. Exploratory students can test the waters by taking classes in a wide variety of topics and won't be required to declare a major until the end of sophomore year. Students who have decided on a major and list this on their application could be offered direct admission to their programs freshman year. We have seven different schools on campus offering direct admission to freshmen. Direct admission is competitive, and only about 10 percent of freshmen will be directly admitted to their intended program freshman year. The other 90 percent are offered general admission to IU and will need to apply to their school at the end of freshman year once they complete the necessary requirements. Students considering majors in the Jacobs School of Music [however] should list music on the application as their intended major. Direct admission to the Jacobs School is a two-tier process that will require a second application to the music school and an audition or interview for prospective students." –Lauren Kay, Assistant Director of Admissions, Indiana University

What should I do now?

At this point, you should have been able to answer some questions about your personality, your academic history, your extracurricular activities, your talents and abilities, and your preferences in the type of college you are looking for. The college search is time consuming and you may feel overloaded with deadlines and all of the small and large tasks you need to complete. The planner on the next several pages will help you keep track of the many deadlines ahead.

Monthly Planner			
Month	*9th Grade*	*10th Grade*	*11th Grade*	*12th Grade*
September	Take challenging classes	Take challenging classes	Take challenging classes	Take a full load of classes
	Take every class seriously	Take every class seriously	Take every class seriously	Take every class seriously
	Attend a club fair featuring clubs and organizations offered in your high school	Attend a club fair featuring clubs and organizations offered in your high school	Attend a club fair featuring clubs and organizations offered in your high school	Meet with your guidance counselor to finalize your college list
	Join clubs, begin activities	Join clubs, begin activities	Join clubs, begin activities	Continue your activities
	READ!	READ!	Take on leadership positions	Prepare for fall SAT/ACT exams
	Remember, every grade counts!	Remember, every grade counts!	Remember, every grade counts!	Send SAT/ACT scores to colleges
	Study in advance for exams	Study in advance for exams	Study in advance for exams	Recheck your academic transcript
	Set small goals	Set small goals	Set small goals	Apply to rolling admissions colleges (see Chapter 3), spaces fill up early
	Try to increase your class participation	Try to increase your class participation	Try to increase your class participation	Visit college campuses
	Review class notes in between classes	Review class notes in between classes	Review class notes in between classes	Check your Facebook and other online profiles and delete any inappropriate material

NOTES: _____

_____

_____

_____

Monthly Planner, continued				
Month	**9th Grade**	**10th Grade**	**11th Grade**	**12th Grade**
October	Get tutoring and attend extra help sessions as needed	Get tutoring and attend extra help sessions as needed	Get tutoring and attend extra help sessions as needed	Check on teachers' letters of recommendations
	Start thinking about possible careers	Take the PSAT exam, if your school offers it	Take the PSAT exam, if your school offers it	Establish a neutral e-mail to put on college applications (discussed in Chapter 6)
	Manage your time wisely	Manage your time wisely	Manage your time wisely	Apply to rolling admissions colleges
	Use an agenda book	Use an agenda book	Use an agenda book	Take SAT/ACT again, if necessary, and send your scores
	READ!	Take the PLAN (pre-ACT) if your school offers it	READ!	Visit college campuses
	Every grade counts	READ!	Every grade counts	Meet with admissions officers visiting your high school, if appropriate
	Set small goals	Start thinking about possible careers	Start thinking about possible careers	Avoid senioritis, stay engaged in school

NOTES: _____

_____

_____

_____

_____

Monthly Planner, continued			
Month	**9th Grade**	**10th Grade**	**11th Grade**	**12th Grade**
November	Visit your guidance counselor	Visit your guidance counselor	Visit your guidance counselor	Early decision and early action application deadlines
	Review your report card/evaluate your performance	Review your report card/evaluate your performance	Review your report card/evaluate your performance	Take the SAT/ACT again, if necessary, and send your scores
	Take appropriate steps if your grades are not where you want them to be: talk to teachers, cut down on computer time	Take appropriate steps if your grades are not where you want them to be: talk to teachers, cut down on computer time	Take appropriate steps if your grades are not where you want them to be: talk to teachers, cut down on computer time	Work on special talent portfolios (art, music, drama, and writing)
	READ!	READ!	Research colleges	Continue to visit colleges
	Increase class participation	Increase class participation	READ!	Work on regular decision applications
	Don't be afraid to ask for help if you need it	Don't be afraid to ask for help if you need it	Don't be afraid to ask for help if you need it	Don't be afraid to ask for help if you need it

NOTES: _____

_____

_____

_____

_____

_____

_____

_____

\	\	\	\	\
Monthly Planner, continued				
Month	*9th Grade*	*10th Grade*	*11th Grade*	*12th Grade*
December	Begin a conversation with your parents about college	Receive and review your PSAT/PLAN scores	Receive and review your PSAT scores	Continue to work on regular decision applications; use a planner or files to organize application
	Continue to read during vacation	Talk to your parents about colleges and financial concerns	Start preparing for SAT/ACT exams	Take SAT/ACT again, if needed
	READ!	READ!	READ!	Some early action, early decision II applications are due; early decision I results are in!
	Use the FAFSA4CASTER at fafsa4caster.ed.gov to project financial aid awards for college	Use the FAFSA4CASTER at fafsa4caster.ed.gov to project financial aid awards for college	Use the FAFSA4CASTER at fafsa4caster.ed.gov to project financial aid awards for college	Remind teachers to complete their letters of recommendation
	Review your teachers' pages on high school's Web site (if it has one) for updates on homework, quizzes, and notes	Review your teachers' pages on high school's Web site (if it has one) for updates on homework, quizzes, and notes	Review your teachers' pages on high school's Web site (if it has one) for updates on homework, quizzes, and notes	Take the SAT/ACT again, if necessary and send your scores
	Take appropriate steps if your grades are not where you want them to be: talk to teachers, cut down on computer time	Take appropriate steps if your grades are not where you want them to be: talk to teachers, cut down on computer time	Take appropriate steps if your grades are not where you want them to be: talk to teachers, cut down on computer time	Check with your guidance counselor to ensure your application documents have been sent
	Try to get to know 1 or 2 teachers on a more personal level	Try to get to know 1 or 2 teachers on a more personal level	Try to get to know 1 or 2 teachers on a more personal level	Review your application status online at college Web sites

NOTES: _____

_____

_____

Monthly Planner, continued			
Month	**9th Grade**	**10th Grade**	**11th Grade**	**12th Grade**
January	Select classes for next year	Select classes for next year	Select classes for next year	Early action decisions start coming in!
	Review your report card/evaluate your performance	Review your report card/evaluate your performance	Review your report card/evaluate your performance	Most regular decision applications are now due
	Take appropriate steps if your grades are not where you want them to be: talk to teachers, cut down on computer time	Take appropriate steps if your grades are not where you want them to be: talk to teachers, cut down on computer time	Register for SAT/ACT exams	Follow up on your applications to make sure they are complete
	READ!	READ!	Prepare for SAT/ACT exams	Complete FAFSA and other financial aid applications
	Start thinking about your plans for the summer	Start thinking about your plans for the summer	Start thinking about your plans for the summer	Research and complete scholarship applications
	Prepare for midterms	Prepare for midterms	Make an appointment with your guidance counselor for your junior meeting to discuss colleges	Complete special talent portfolios

NOTES: _____

_____

_____

_____

_____

_____

_____

Monthly Planner, continued				
Month	*9th Grade*	*10th Grade*	*11th Grade*	*12th Grade*
February	Get tutoring and attend extra help sessions, as needed	Get tutoring and attend extra help sessions, as needed	Get tutoring and attend extra help sessions, as needed	Get tutoring and attend extra help sessions, as needed
	Use your time wisely	Use your time wisely	Use your time wisely	Continue doing well in your classes
	Continue your involvement in school and outside activities	Continue your involvement in school and outside activities	Continue your involvement in school and outside activities	Follow up on your applications to make sure they are complete and update regular decision schools about new activities
	READ!	READ!	Prepare for SAT/ACT exams	Complete FAFSA and other financial aid applications
	Start thinking about your plans for the summer	It's never too early to start researching colleges	Register for spring SAT/ACT exams	Early action decisions are coming in!
	Remember, every grade counts	Remember, every grade counts	Start attending college fairs	Complete special talent portfolios

NOTES: _____

_____

_____

_____

_____

_____

_____

_____

Monthly Planner, continued			
Month	**9th Grade**	**10th Grade**	**11th Grade**	**12th Grade**
March	Visit your guidance counselor	Visit your guidance counselor	Prepare for SAT/ACT exams	Regular decision results start coming in!
	READ!	READ!	Register for spring SAT/ACT exams	Avoid senioritis
	Prepare in advance for exams	Prepare in advance for exams	Visit college campuses	Revisit colleges
	Review daily, rather than cramming for exams	Review daily, rather than cramming for exams	Research college Web sites and other relevant sites	Decision time is coming; review which college is the best fit for you
	Perform community service or volunteer at a place of interest (local vet/animal shelter, nursing home, after school program...)	Perform community service or volunteer at a place of interest (local vet/animal shelter, nursing home, after school program...)	Perform community service or volunteer at a place of interest (local vet/animal shelter, nursing home, after school program...)	Look for scholar-ships from local organizations, check with your guidance counselor for ideas
	Improve your vocab-ulary and reading comprehension skills	Improve your vocab-ulary and reading comprehension skills	Improve your vocab-ulary and reading comprehension skills	Think about worth-while summer activities
	Try to get to know 1 or 2 teachers on a more personal level	Try to get to know 1 or 2 teachers on a more personal level	Try to get to know 1 or 2 teachers on a more personal level	Review your appli-cation status online at college Web sites
	Do your homework—stay motivated	Do your homework—stay motivated	Do your homework—stay motivated	Do your homework—stay motivated

NOTES: _____

_____

_____

_____

_____

Month	9th Grade	10th Grade	11th Grade	12th Grade
		Monthly Planner, continued		
April	Review your report card and evaluate your progress	Review your report card and evaluate your progress	Review your report card and evaluate your progress	Regular decision results are coming in!
	Take appropriate steps if grades are not where you want them to be	Take appropriate steps if grades are not where you want them to be	Take appropriate steps if grades are not where you want them to be	Continue doing well in your classes
	Start thinking about your plans for the summer	Start thinking about your plans for the summer	Ask at least two teachers for letters of recommendation	Revisit colleges on your short list to help you finalize your decision
	READ!	READ!	Prepare for SAT/ACT exams	Write thank you notes to teachers and counselor
	It's never too early to start researching colleges	It's never too early to start researching colleges	Register for spring SAT/ACT exams	Avoid senioritis, senior grades still count!
	Reread class notes	Reread class notes	Attend open houses and college fairs	Talk to your parents about your final decision

NOTES: _____

_____

_____

_____

_____

_____

_____

_____

Monthly Planner, continued			
Month	*9th Grade*	*10th Grade*	*11th Grade*	*12th Grade*
May	READ!	Take Advanced Placement exams, if you are in AP classes	Take Advanced Placement exams, if you are in AP classes	Take Advanced Placement exams, if you are in AP classes
	Continue with extracurricular activities	Continue with extracurricular activities	Take SAT/ACT exams	May 1—universal reply date
	Cut down on computer and TV time	Cut down on computer and TV time	Visit college campuses	Send only one deposit to the college you will be attending
	Set small goals; don't feel overwhelmed	Set small goals; don't feel overwhelmed	Attend open houses and college fairs	Notify colleges you have decided not to attend
	Reduce test anxiety: be prepared, take practice tests, and use relaxation techniques	Reduce test anxiety: be prepared, take practice tests, and use relaxation techniques	Reduce test anxiety: be prepared, take practice tests, and use relaxation techniques	Reduce test anxiety: be prepared, take practice tests, and use relaxation techniques
	Use your time wisely!	Set aside 15 minutes daily for personal reading	Set aside 15 minutes daily for personal reading	Complete housing forms and relevant papers
	Talk to family and friends about potential careers	Talk to family and friends about potential careers	Talk to family and friends about potential careers	Talk to family and friends about potential careers

NOTES: _____

_____

_____

_____

_____

_____

\	Monthly Planner, continued			
Month	**9th Grade**	**10th Grade**	**11th Grade**	**12th Grade**
June	Study for finals	Study for finals	Study for finals	Study for finals
	Finalize your plans for the summer	Finalize your plans for the summer	Review your academic transcript	Waitlist decisions start arriving from colleges that are still considering you
	Review your end of year report card and evaluate your performance	Review your end of year report card and evaluate your performance	Review your end of year report card and evaluate your performance	Review your end of year report card and evaluate your performance
	Jot down your activities for the year to start building your resume	Jot down your activities for the year to start building your resume	Jot down your activities for the year to start building your resume	Say goodbye to friends and teachers
	Set small goals; don't feel overwhelmed	Set small goals; don't feel overwhelmed	Take last SAT/ACT of the school year	GRADUATION DAY has finally arrived!

NOTES: _____

_____

_____

_____

_____

_____

_____

_____

_____

_____

Monthly Planner, continued			
Month	**9th Grade**	**10th Grade**	**11th Grade**	**12th Grade**
July	Continue to read!	Continue to read!	Continue to read! Do something challenging over the summer	Continue to read!
	Talk to your parents about college	It's not too early to start visiting colleges	Visit colleges	Attend orientation sessions
	Begin summer activities	Begin summer activities	Start working on your college essay and resume	Register for fall classes
	Shadow/spend a day (or more) with people in careers that interest you	Shadow/spend a day (or more) with people in careers that interest you	Shadow/spend a day (or more) with people in careers that interest you	Take a summer course at a community college for college credit
	Don't procrastinate summer reading assignments, if you have one	Don't procrastinate summer reading assignments, if you have one	Don't procrastinate summer reading assignments, if you have one	Make a list of items you'll need for college
	If you travel, keep a photo journal for a potential college essay	If you travel, keep a photo journal for a potential college essay	If you travel, keep a photo journal for a potential college essay	Make the most of your last summer before college!

NOTES: _____

_____

_____

_____

_____

_____

_____

Monthly Planner, continued				
Month	**9th Grade**	**10th Grade**	**11th Grade**	**12th Grade**
August	Continue to read!	Continue to read!	Visit colleges	Attend orientation sessions and register for fall classes
	Prepare for another year of high school	Prepare for another year of school	Get organized! Download or view applications and start working on them	College classes finally begin!
	Save money for college—babysit, get a part-time job, etc.	Save money for college—babysit, get a part-time job, etc.	Save money for college—babysit, get a part-time job, etc.	Save money for college—babysit, get a part-time job, etc.
	Volunteer for a worthwhile organization	Volunteer for a worthwhile organization	Volunteer for a worthwhile organization	Volunteer for a worthwhile organization
	Shop for school supplies	Shop for school supplies	Shop for school supplies	Shop for supplies for college
	Get organized and set goals for what you want to achieve this school year	Get organized and set goals for what you want to achieve this school year	Get organized and set goals for what you want to achieve this school year	Get organized and set goals for what you want to achieve this school year

NOTES: _____

_____

_____

_____

_____

_____

_____

_____

How You're Judged: What College Admissions Officers Look For

66I look for the quality of the applicant's curriculum. In other words, did the applicant take the most challenging program offered at his/her high school and did he/she experience success?

Will the applicant make a positive contribution to the university community academically and socially? What will we learn from this applicant?99

–Mitchell L. Thompson Jr., Dean of Students, Scarsdale High School;
Former Associate Dean of Admissions and Records at The Cooper Union;
and Former Admissions Director for SUNY Oneonta

Different types of colleges look for different factors in an applicant. A public university may place more of an emphasis on *objective factors,* including grades, academic program, and standardized test scores. A private university may look at objective factors as well as some *subjective factors,* including essays, extracurricular activities, legacy (whether either of your parents attended the college), teacher and counselor letters of recommendations, and others. More competitive public universities also look at subjective factors. This use of objective and subjective admission factors is known as a *holistic approach,* where many indicators are taken into account when reviewing your application. A very selective college, private or public, looks at many more admissions factors than a less selective college.

In general, colleges look for students who they believe will succeed in college. Which factors do they use to gauge how successful you will be? Your academic average or GPA (Grade Point Average) is the most important indicator of how well you will perform in college. According to the National Association of College Admissions Counselors' (NACAC) State of College Admission 2008 Report, the four top factors used by most colleges are your

- grades in college preparatory classes
- academic program (what classes you have taken)

- SAT/ACT scores
- overall GPA

The next set of factors that are considered are personal statements, essays, class rank (if given), letters of recommendations, extracurricular activities, your demonstrated interest in attending a school, subject test scores (if needed), and interviews (if needed). *Demonstrated interest* is a measure of how interested you are in a university, and usually includes whether you have joined a college's mailing list, requested viewbooks or other materials, visited campus on an official tour, attended open houses or information sessions, or had any correspondence with admissions officers.

How do colleges view the philosophy of admissions?

The philosophy of how to build a freshman class varies widely from college to college and sometimes from year to year. For example, if a college needs a football player or an oboist to round out their team or orchestra, and you happen to play that sport or that musical instrument, then you may have a leg up on the competition.

Many colleges post their philosophy of the admissions process on their Web site. When you become interested in a college, you should try to determine what their philosophy is to see if you fit into their parameters. For example, the New York University (NYU) Web site states that NYU is looking to form a "geographically, socially, ethnically and economically diverse" class. It goes on to explain what qualities NYU is looking for in an applicant, including motivation, leadership skills, and compassion. They look at a broad range of indicators from a strong pool of applicants to build an "academically talented" and diverse freshman class.

Rice University has a clearly stated philosophy of what type of student they want to admit. They explain that they use standardized test scores "cautiously" and that they use a "broader perspective" with the goal of "enriching the learning environment at Rice."

Here's what our panel of admissions experts tells us regarding the most significant factors they look for in an applicant.

NYU Philosophy

A large and exceptionally well-qualified applicant pool enables us to enroll a freshman class that is academically talented as well as remarkably diverse. Recognizing that each applicant offers a unique combination of achievements and potential, we carefully consider the entire application.

–Excerpt from the NYU Web site

Rice University's Mission Statement

We seek a broadly diverse student body where educational diversity increases the intellectual vitality of education, scholarship, service and communal life at Rice . . . We endeavor to craft a residential community that fosters creative, inter-cultural interactions among students, a place where prejudices of all sorts are confronted squarely and dispelled.

–Excerpt from the Rice University Web site

Nancy J. Maly, Director of Admissions, Grinnell College, stresses the following factors:

- Strong academic preparation for college
- Interest in and understanding of Grinnell College
- Potential to contribute to the institution in meaningful ways
- Interests/activities, both academic and personal, that suggest a potential match with the college

Raymond Lutzky, Director of Outreach, Rensselaer Polytechnic Institute, looks for:

- Strong performance in high school, particularly in math and science.
- Well-rounded with outside interests/involvement, such as athletics, church involvement, volunteer commitments, student or other civic organizations.
- Entrepreneurial spirit: "Many students have started their own companies before they even enter Rensselaer, such as Karthik Bala '97, founder of Vicarious Visions, the company that makes *Guitar Hero*. While most high schools do not teach entrepreneurship, we like to see some interest from the student in commericialization, product design, or running their own small business."
- Background/diversity brought to the student body: "At Rensselaer, we are looking for students from all walks of life, all socio-economic conditions, all cultures, religions and races. Students with unique backgrounds (everything from an Iowa farm to an Indonesian city) always add to the total Rensselaer community."

Lauren A. Kay, Assistant Director of Admissions, Indiana University, says,

- "The most significant factors are grades and grade trends, the strength of a student's courses, and test scores."

Cheryl Brown, Director of Undergraduate Admissions, Binghamton University, State University of New York, says,

- "Binghamton uses a holistic approach to reading applications. What this means is that you're more than just a number and test scores. We look at extracurricular activities, interests and consider other factors. That doesn't mean that grades and academic performance aren't important—they are! Binghamton is a top public university and our students' academic performances reflect that. We admit high achieving, well rounded students, who graduate Binghamton ready to succeed professionally and personally."

How do colleges read applications?

There are various ways in which colleges read your application. Some city and state universities set minimum GPAs and standardized test scores and then in some cases a computer determines whether you have met the minimum qualifications for admission. More selective universities have a multistep process. The University of Michigan, for example, clearly posts its process for reading applications and its freshman rating sheet on its Web site. The process at the University of Michigan and at many other colleges is that there are at least two holistic reviews completed for each applicant. There is an initial reader, who reviews your file and makes a determination to admit or reject. Your file is then reviewed by a second reader and he or she makes an independent assessment of your admission status. The file is then given to an assistant director who may agree with the first two readers or he or she can bring your file to the attention of a committee for its last review for a final decision.

Many colleges have a two-reader process. Some colleges have counselors who read for a specific region, others just have general readers. Applicants who are clear-cut for admission or rejection may not go before a committee for a final review. At these committee meetings, counselors discuss in detail the merits of your application, taking into account your grades, standardized test scores, academic program, reputation of your high school, extracurricular activities, essays, teachers and counselor recommendations, and other admission criteria.

The University of Michigan's rating system targets seven areas as follows, which should give you an idea of how many complex factors some colleges take into account when evaluating applicants.

University of Michigan's Rating System	
Secondary school academic performance	Recalculated GPA
	Quality of high school curriculum
	Test scores
	Academic interests
	Class rank
	Other
Educational environment	Strength of curriculum (honors, AP, IB courses offered)
	Average SAT/ACT scores
	Percent attending four-year colleges
	Grading system
	Academically disadvantaged school

Counselor and teacher recommendations	Character
	Civic and cultural awareness
	Commitment to high ideals
	Intellectual independence/enthusiasm for learning/ risk taking
	Creative/artistic talent
	Concern for others
	Motivation/determination/effort
	Leadership potential/maturity/responsibility
Personal background	Cultural awareness/experiences
	Socioeconomic and educational background (including first generation to attend college)
	Geographic considerations (including underrepresented geographic areas)
	Awards/honors
	Extracurricular activities, service and leadership
	Participation in enrichment or outreach activities
	Alumni relationships
	Scholarship athlete
	Work experience
	Other (military, other types of service)
Evaluative measures	Depth in academic area of student's interest
	Evidence of academic passion
	Grasp of world events
	Intellectual curiosity
	Artistic talent
	Writing quality
Extenuating circumstances	Overcoming adversity/unusual hardships
	Language spoken at home
	Frequent moves, attending many different schools
Other considerations	Demonstrated interest in college/good match
	Strong personal statement

How the Colleges Represented by Our Panel of Admissions Experts Read Applications

Admissions counselors and directors share with us how their colleges read applications: "Each applicant is reviewed on the basis of academic talent and contributions to our pluralistic campus community. An initial review is done by the recruiter for the geographic area within which the student resides, and then the committee reviews each application holistically."–Cheryl Brown, Director of Undergraduate Admissions, Binghamton University, State University of New York

"The faculties from both the schools of art and architecture made the creative decisions. The admissions office had a say about the academic strengths of the applicants. For engineering, the admissions office made the decision. Often, the school the applicant applied from played a role in the decision as well. An 'A' in one school is not an 'A' in another. And gender, race, ethnicity, geography, and extracurricular activities played an important role in making a positive decision."–Mitchell Thompson, Dean of Students, Scarsdale HS, former Associate Dean of Admissions and Records, The Cooper Union

"They review each applicant individually and we make decisions based on each student's merits, regardless of the student's major, geographic area, or high school. If each student from a particular high school is admissible, we'll admit all of them! We don't cap the number of students we'll admit from each school."–Lauren Kay, Assistant Director, Indiana University

"The review looks at academic preparation/level of success in the secondary school program, standardized test scores, and for other evidence (talents/interests/extra or co-curricular activities) that suggest an applicant can be successful and happy. Readers review applications by region which correlates with their recruitment travel. This brings a personal knowledge of the applicants' schools/programs into the review process.

After first review, a second review is done by someone who typically does not know the region. If both readers evaluate the application similarly, the review is finished. If the first and second reviews produce disparate evaluations, applications get a third review by a selection committee. One final review is done to shape the entering class. If there are multiple applicants from the same school, the group's results are collected and reviewed to make sure that an applicant has not been under- or overrated vis-à-vis the peer group."–Nancy J. Maly, Director of Admission, Grinnell College

"Rensselaer reads applications electronically via committee. We do indicate whether other students from a particular high school have applied, along with demographic data."–Raymond Lutzky, Director of Outreach, Rensselaer Polytechnic Institute

What is my academic average and class rank?

As you have already read, your academic average or GPA is one of the most important criteria that colleges consider when reviewing your application. Although the format varies widely from high school to high school, the high school you attend sends a transcript of your work in ninth, tenth, and eleventh grades. Colleges review your application and make decisions based on three-year's worth of academic classes. Some high schools run on a semester schedule, others use trimesters and still others use block schedules. *Block scheduling* is a type of course programming where classes do not meet every day. Classes meet for longer periods a few times a week so students can focus more intently on these subjects.

There are high schools that use weighted averages and some that use unweighted averages. For schools using *weighted averages,* challenging courses such as Honors, Advanced Placement, College level, or International Baccalaureate (IB) courses receive extra weight. It is possible for students to attain more than a 100 average or a 4.0 GPA. There are students who graduate with averages of 120 or more on a 100-point scale or a 5.0 GPA on a 4.0 scale. In schools where *unweighted averages* are used, each class counts equally. Students can graduate with no more than a 100 average on a 100-point scale or no more than a 4.0 on a 4.0 scale. There are also high schools which submit both weighted and unweighted averages. Due to the varying methods used in calculating GPAs, some colleges unweight a weighted average, and some schools recalculate your GPA in order to equalize all applicants and to compare one high school to another high school.

You may be wondering how colleges know what grading policy your high school uses, and, as you can imagine, it can be very confusing at times. High schools typically send a "High School Profile," which explains the grading policy of your school and other information about your graduating class, including standardized test scores, how many students are in your class, how many attend four-year colleges, whether or not your school ranks students, and what types of courses your school offers.

Then there is the issue of class rank. More and more high schools are moving away from ranking students, so check with your high school to find out your school's policy. Although it sounds good in theory, class rank can actually hurt students. For example, in a very small graduating class of 50 students, the top 10 percent (the highest performing students in the school) of the class only includes five students. If you are ranked as the tenth student in the class, you can still have a very high average. If you are in a large graduating class of 500 students and you are ranked number 200, you could still be a 90+ student. It would appear that you are not doing well when in fact you have a very admirable average. Class rank can work to a student's disadvantage, which is why some high schools are moving away from using it. Instead of using class rank, which could be misleading, some high schools indicate percentiles (top 10%, 20%, and so forth) to give colleges an idea of where you are in the graduating class. Other high schools do not use any type of ranking system or class percentiles. Colleges usually ask for the highest average in the class, so they can get a sense of where you are in comparison. Your high school's policy about class rank is its to set, but you should be aware of the policy.

How will colleges view my transcript?

A high school transcript is carefully scrutinized by college admissions counselors. Your transcript is your academic record of your ninth, tenth, and eleventh grade accomplishments. College counselors look at your overall GPA and your record in college preparatory classes. Transcripts vary in their appearance and content. In some high schools across the country, your grades on a state assessment are included on your transcript, such as the Regents exams in New York State.

In viewing your academic record, admissions counselors are looking for trends and how successful you have been in your course work. Are your grades fairly consistent year to year? Are your grades on an upward or downward curve? An upward curve may indicate that your work ethic has improved and you are maturing; colleges like to see this trend. A downward curve (especially senior year) may not be a positive sign. If there are any reasons for any inconsistencies in grades or a downward trend, you may want to give an explanation in an essay or in the additional information section on the application. There are some legitimate reasons why your grades may be erratic, including illness, divorce, or other personal situations. If there is a legitimate explanation (other than laziness), your guidance counselor can indicate in his or her letter of recommendation that you have an extenuating circumstance. Colleges may or may not be sympathetic, but at least they know what transpired in your high school career. Take an objective look at your transcript; determine whether you have performed consistently and whether you have any positive or negative trends, and you see what colleges see when reviewing your academic record.

> **TIP:** At the end of each academic year and especially before your college applications are sent in your senior year, check your transcript for such things as incorrect grades, missing grades, or any mistakes.

What types of courses should I take?

In addition to viewing grades, admissions counselors are looking at what type of academic program you have taken in high school. Colleges do expect students to challenge themselves and not to take just "fluff" courses. Most universities recommend that you complete 4 years of English, 3 years of social studies or history, 3 years of math, 3 years of science, and at least 2 years of a foreign language plus the required electives that your state and high school require. More selective colleges expect you to take 4 years of English, 4 years of social studies, 4 years of science, 4 years of math, and 3 years of a foreign language, plus electives.

> **TIP:** Attempt challenging courses. If your school doesn't offer what you want, take a summer or evening class at a local community college. Your initiative and desire to challenge yourself beyond what your high school offers make you a better candidate.

If your high school offers honors, Advanced Placement (AP), college level (courses offered through a local university), or IB courses and you believe you can do well in them, you should go ahead and take these classes (in some high schools you may need to be recommended by a teacher or chairperson). If, however, you attend a school where these accelerated courses are not offered, you are not penalized for not taking these classes.

One of the most common questions that students ask guidance counselors is, "Should I take honors or accelerated courses, such as AP, college level, or IB courses?" The answer is a qualified yes. If you have been recommended or if you have open enrollment (anyone can take these classes) for these courses and you believe you can succeed (mid 80s range and above), then yes, you should take these challenging courses. If you think that just being in an accelerated course and barely passing or attaining 70s is going to impress a college admissions person, then you are mistaken.

Another commonly asked question is, "Is it better to get a 'B' (80s or above) in an accelerated course or an 'A' (90 or above) in a regular class?" The answer is that most colleges would prefer that you take rigorous courses and do well in them. The more selective universities answer that they expect 'A's or 90s in all accelerated courses. If you attend a high school where you are not tracked and you can take whatever classes best suit you, then you should play to your strengths. If you are a strong math and science student and an average or below-average English and history student, then you should focus on advanced classes in your areas of strength. The reverse is also true for students whose strengths lie in English and social studies. If you are an all-around good student, then you should attempt challenging courses in as many areas as possible.

Remember, if your high school does not offer any advanced courses, you are not hurt by this in any way. However, if you have an opportunity to take a summer or evening class at a local community college or university, your initiative is viewed positively.

Taking Challenging Courses: Advice from Admission Counselors

"Rensselaer is very supportive of accelerated coursework, AP and IB exams. Students should check with their universities before deciding whether or not to load up on these courses—after all, there is no 'AP arms race' between students. One of the key elements in a student's application to Rensselaer should be that they thrive in a challenging environment. If a student sails through nonhonors classes in hopes of achieving straight 'A's, it may impact them negatively during the admissions process. It is not uncommon for straight 'A' students to arrive at Rensselaer and receive their first 'B's or 'C's. Being able to deal with a challenging academic environment is a very important skill for students to learn. A balance between strong academic coursework and grades to raise a curriculum average is the way to go, in my opinion. Allowing students to sail through easy coursework in hopes of a higher GPA will set the student up for failure at a tougher selective college." –Raymond Lutzky, Director of Outreach, Rensselaer Polytechnic Institute

continued

continued

"Competitive institutions expect to see evidence that applicants challenge themselves. If accelerated AP or IB courses are offered, there is an expectation that the student will have taken some. Students should always take courses at, or slightly beyond, the upper limit of their academic ability. Stellar grades in unchallenging courses are unimpressive. The entire program of study is examined." –Nancy J. Maly, Director of Admission, Grinnell College

"Indiana encourages students to challenge themselves by taking honors and AP classes, but we don't want to see students struggle in these higher level classes. If a student is taking honors and AP classes, we'll expect that he/she is earning above average grades in these classes." –Lauren Kay, Assistant Director, Indiana University–Bloomington

"Binghamton is looking for students who take accelerated courses, so you should take classes that challenge you. Advanced classes provide you with a wonderful foundation for moving into college coursework. We look at the course, course level and the grade—not just the grade. Advanced courses demonstrate taking on the academic challenge, not just aiming for an exceptional grade. That being said, the best scenario of course, is an advanced class that results in an outstanding grade!" –Cheryl Brown, Director of Undergraduate Admission, Binghamton University, State University of New York

"If accelerated and AP courses are offered, then the student should challenge themselves by taking them. Colleges can tell the quality of a particular program, let's say the AP program, based on how many students over a period of years earn 4s or 5s. I'd rather see a 'B+' in an honors level course than an 'A' in a regular level course. Here's the reality: If a student is applying to a very competitive university, then the students should take the most challenging courses offered and do well. That's the real answer." –Mitchell Thompson, Dean of Students, Scarsdale High School and former Associate Dean of Admissions and Records, The Cooper Union

How important are standardized tests?

Standardized tests have grown in importance over the last 10 to 15 years, and, as a result, many students feel pressured to do well on these tests. The two standardized tests involved in the college admissions process are the SAT, administered by the College Board, and the ACT, administered by the American College Testing program. The original value of these exams was to be able to predict a student's first-year college grades. After extensive studies, it appears that there may be some gender, cultural, and economic biases inherent in both tests, which is one of the reasons why testing is a controversial topic.

Unfortunately, I have seen students with high averages, great essays, and outstanding extracurricular activities turned away by the college of their choice because of disappointing test scores. Parents, also disappointed by their child's test scores, naively ask whether the colleges can overlook this one area and optimistically hope that high grades, a great essay, or extracurricular activities can outweigh lower test scores. Colleges that practice holistic admissions policies may weigh other factors in addition to testing scores. There is a growing wave of concern over how heavily these scores are being used and in what ways these scores are being used. For very selective schools (with some exceptions), standardized test scores continue to be among the top factors used for admission purposes.

Standardized test scores, in addition to being a factor in the admissions process, are also used for evaluation for scholarship purposes, including individual state scholarship programs.

Are there any testing-optional colleges or universities?

As a result of the deepening concern over the testing frenzy, several organizations have arisen to address the testing issue. If you have difficulty attaining the score you want or need in order to attend the college(s) of your choice, do not despair! There are over 800 colleges that are testing-optional, meaning that you do not have to submit your test scores in order to be considered, even by very selective colleges. More colleges are added to the list each year. For a complete list of testing-optional colleges, visit fairtest.org. Keep in mind that in lieu of standardized test scores, some of these testing-optional colleges may require SAT Subject Tests, graded essays, or other criteria to replace test scores. In some cases, test scores won't be used for admission purposes but could be used to place you in the proper level of your classes. Some testing-optional colleges also use test scores to determine merit scholarships, so you may have to submit test scores to be considered for some scholarships. It is important to carefully research the policies of each testing-optional college before you apply.

Sample of Testing-Optional Colleges

University of Arizona, AZ	Hartwick College, NY
Pitzer College, CA	Sarah Lawrence College, NY
Connecticut College, CT	School of The Visual Arts, NY
Hampshire College, MA	Franklin & Marshall, PA
Goucher College, MD	Gettysburg College, PA
Bowdoin College, ME	Muhlenberg College, PA
Wake Forest College, NC	Providence College, RI
Bard College, NY	George Mason University, VA
Fashion Institute of Technology, NY	Benington College, VT
Hamilton College, NY	

What are the differences between the SAT and the ACT?

Since the reality is that standardized test scores are so important in the admissions process, how do you decide which test is right for you? The SAT is taken by more students on the East Coast, because that is where the College Board is located (NY and NJ). The ACT is taken by more students on the West Coast, because the administrator of the exam is located in Iowa. More and more students on both coasts are trying the other test. The SAT has historically been known as an *aptitude test,* whereas the ACT is more of an *achievement* or *content-based* test. An aptitude test usually measures future potential, and the concepts being assessed are more abstract. An achievement or content-based test measures achievement in current course work

> **TIP:** There is no harm in taking both the SAT and the ACT and seeing which test you like better. You can also take a sample SAT/ACT to see which test works best for you.

and is therefore more closely aligned with the curriculum being learned. Since the introduction of the Writing section on the SAT a few years ago, the SAT is now 3 hours 45 minutes, not including administrative tasks (completing the answer sheet, breaks, etc.). The ACT is slightly shorter with the optional Writing section: 3 hours, 25 minutes, plus administrative tasks.

Much research has been conducted on these two tests. Students who are studiers and more concrete thinkers may perform better on the ACT. As research results vary, a good practice is to discuss the merits of both tests with your guidance counselor. There is no disadvantage to trying both tests one time and then deciding for yourself which one is better suited for you.

Because taking the ACT's Writing section is optional, always check with the college you are considering to see if it is required. As of this writing, many colleges do not use the writing section of the SAT or ACT in the admissions process. Some highly competitive schools review this section, though, so check the college's Web site for exact instructions on testing. You should be aware that there is the potential for colleges to view and compare your essay portion of either test with your personal statement from the application.

COMPARISON OF SAT/ACT EXAMS		
Criteria	*SAT*	*ACT*
Type of test	Aptitude Predictive	Achievement Content-based, related to high school curriculum
Timing	3 hours, 45 minutes plus administrative time	3 hours, 25 minutes (including ACT Writing Test) plus administrative time
Content	Critical reading, math, writing	English, math, reading, science, writing (optional)
Sections	10 (includes one experimental section)	5
Scoring	200–800 per section Overall score of 2,400 with three sections 0–12 on essay	1–36 per section Overall composite score 0–12 on essay
Penalties	No penalty for omitted questions ¼ pt. deduction for wrong answers on multiple choice questions	No penalty for wrong/omitted answers Guessing is encouraged

Another aspect of testing to consider is when and how often to test. When to test really depends on when you are ready to take the test and whether you have too much on your plate (other exams, including APs, finals, state assessments) during testing time. The SAT is usually offered seven times a year and the ACT is usually offered six times a year (neither is offered in July or August). Students typically take these tests between one to three times and occasionally four or more times. When you test is up to you and your guidance counselor. There is a myth that the curve for these exams is different in different months, but this is not accurate. So, take the test when you feel most ready. There is some evidence that your peak test scores could occur in the fall of your senior year, so do not be afraid to repeat the tests in the October–January administration (up to November for most early decision schools.)

Many colleges attempt to put the student in the best light possible, and one way to do this is to mix and match scores from different administrations of the SAT. An emerging trend is to "superscore" the ACT, which basically means to mix and match subtest scores to form a new composite (overall) score. Other colleges mix and match ACT and SAT scores to form the highest reading score and the highest math score from both exams. Since policies vary widely from college to college, always check the college's Web site or ask an admissions counselor. There is so much variation in policies it is no wonder that students and parents are confused by the process!

Sample of Colleges that Superscore the ACT

Amherst College	University of Miami
Beloit University	University of South Florida
University of Colorado–Boulder	Stanford University
University of Dayton	Washington & Lee University
Elon University	Washington University
George Washington University	
Georgia Tech University	
Indiana University	
Northeastern University	
Pepperdine University	

There is a lot of confusion over the testing process. The myth that there are different curves for each test administration is not true. Take the test when you feel ready. Talk to your guidance counselor about any questions you have.

How do I prepare for the SAT/ACT?

One of the controversies associated with the SAT/ACT is that students can be coached to improve their scores. Many studies have been conducted to determine if coaching actually improves students' scores, but the results are not conclusive. It is really up to you and your parents to determine if you have the time and the financial resources to obtain formal preparation services.

Millions, even billions, of dollars are spent every year on preparing for these exams; preparation can include books, online courses, group classes, and private tutors. Some preparation is suggested, but how to best prepare depends on the individual student and the student's level of motivation. Spending a lot of money is not a guarantee of a large increase in test scores. Some students are helped by test preparation and others are not. What is helpful, though, is to take multiple practice tests to ensure you understand the directions and the types of questions and to determine what test-taking strategies work best for you. What definitely helps you improve your critical reading scores on both tests is *to read*—everything and anything. From personal experience, I can tell you that many high school students don't read as much as they should. Reading can improve your vocabulary and your reading comprehension. Daily reading for 20 to 30 minutes is in your best interest. A fun way to keep track of the books you read is to open a "Good Reads" account at www.goodreads.com or a similar Web site, www.librarything.com. You can communicate with friends and authors, write book reviews, categorize your books, and recommend books to others. Other fun ways to improve vocabulary and reading comprehension are to play word games, such as crossword puzzles. Online games include www.freerice.com (which also raises funds for underdeveloped countries) and Text Twist, among others.

If you are considering a course or a private tutor, you need to click with the instructor. If you are taking a prep course and are not happy with your instructor or tutor, let the company know and request a different instructor. If you are a very motivated student, you could do perfectly well with a book or an online course. If

> **TIP:** Increase your daily reading and take a lot of practice exams. Look for fun ways to improve your vocabulary and reading comprehension skills.

you need someone to sit on you (figuratively speaking) in order to get you to prepare, then you might be better off with a course or a tutor. The bottom line is that you can prepare to some extent, but you and your parents are the best judge of which method works well for you and with the financial resources available.

Do I need to take subject tests?

Subject tests are hour-long multiple choice tests, administered by the College Board, that test your mastery in a subject area. They are available in five areas:

- English (Literature)
- History (World and U.S.)

- Math (Level 1 and Level 2)
- Science (Biology—Ecological or Molecular—Chemistry, and Physics)
- Languages (Chinese, French, German, Spanish, and Hebrew).

The scoring for a subject test is the same as for the SAT Reasoning Test: 200–800. Selective colleges use subject test scores for admissions purposes and/or for placement in college courses. Some colleges accept your ACT scores in place of subject tests, another good reason to take the ACT. Check college Web sites to determine which ones substitute ACT scores for subject tests.

The best time to take a subject test is after you complete a year's course in the subject. For example, if you take AP Biology in your junior year, then you should take the SAT Biology subject test in June, after you have completed the course. Since the subject tests are based on your high school curriculum, you can prepare for them; studying definitely helps in achieving a respectable grade. If you are not sure if you are applying to a college that requires them, you can still plan on taking the subject tests in courses where you have taken honors or accelerated courses or in areas where you believe your strengths lie. Colleges that do not require a subject test do not count them but they see that you have challenged yourself by attempting the test. If you do not do well on these tests, the colleges that do not require subject tests do not hold it against you. As with the SAT, you can repeat these tests as necessary to raise your score and then you can send the scores to the colleges that require them.

Sample of Colleges that Require SAT Subject Tests

All Ivy League Colleges (Brown, Columbia, Cornell, Dartmouth, Harvard, Princeton, University of Pennsylvania, and Yale)	Duke University
	Emory University
	New York University
Boston University	Pomona College
Brandeis University	Rice University
Bryn Mawr College	Tufts University
California Institute of Technology	University of California
Carnegie Mellon University	University of Virginia
Connecticut College	Washington & Lee University
The Cooper Union	Williams College

How important is the personal statement?

The personal statement or essay is your opportunity to tell college admissions counselors something about yourself that is not readily apparent from your application. It is a subjective factor, and one of the few ways you can communicate even indirectly with counselors to give them a feel for your personality, values, and passion. With the right essay, you can make your presence felt and convey to the reader a sense of who you are and what you care about. It is a vital part of the application and it is one of the few areas in which you have control. At this point in the application process, your grades and standardized test scores are already fixed, so the essay is your chance to set yourself apart from others and to clearly convey why you deserve a place in the college(s) of your choice.

> **TIP:** The essay is a critical part of many applications; take the time to write a great essay.

The importance of the essay varies from college to college. Its value increases at the more selective colleges. Do not underestimate the power of the essay! I know of one admissions director at a large state university who was so swayed by a student's essay that the student was admitted on the spot, even though her grades and SAT scores were slightly below their average admissions standards! Chapter 5 gives you a detailed look at how to write an effective personal essay, but please remember that this is one aspect of the admissions process that is definitely within your power, so take the time to write a convincing personal statement.

How are extracurricular activities viewed?

Any activity that you engage in inside or outside of school is considered an extracurricular activity. Most colleges ask you to list these activities on an application or to attach a brag sheet, a résumé, or an extracurricular activities list, all of these terms being interchangeable.

In addition to selecting candidates based on academic promise and ability, college admissions counselors are looking for students who have contributed their time and leadership skills to their school and to their community. No one ever tells you what clubs to join or what

> **TIP:** If your high school does not offer a club in which you're interested, ask if you can start a new one. Colleges value your initiative and leadership potential.

organizations in which you should become involved. Instead, colleges are hoping that you develop one or two areas of interest, about which you are passionate. It could be sports, music, politics, theatre, creative writing, community service, or any other area in which you excel. College admissions counselors are not generally impressed with a three-page résumé of many different activities, but rather how you have developed your interest or passion throughout high school. Have you added depth to your interest area(s) by progressing to a leadership position? For example, if you joined Key Club (a national organization) in ninth grade, did you become more active by becoming the membership co-chair in tenth grade; then in eleventh grade become a vice president of the club; and then become president and attend the national convention in twelfth grade? These emerging leadership roles show how you have progressed in the organization and further developed your interest level.

Do not attempt to join every organization or club in ninth grade, then drop them and add new clubs every year. Instead, try to develop a few areas of expertise and build on them over time. If your high school does not offer a club you're interested in, then write a proposal and start a new club! If you're interested in becoming a nurse, you can volunteer in your local hospital or shadow someone in the health sciences profession. Use your imagination and your resources to develop and refine your interests. Colleges are interested in what you do with your spare time and they want individuals who bring a fresh perspective and expertise to their campus.

Becoming involved in school or outside of school will make you a more interesting person and an appealing college student. Focusing on a few areas of interest is more desirable than overextending yourself in many different directions and appearing unfocused and spreading yourself too thin. Chapter 6 assists you in developing an effective brag sheet or résumé.

How do colleges view summer and other experiences?

What you do in the summer is somewhat of a controversial topic. Some students and their families believe that students need time off from school and that the summer is a time for fun and may include attending or working in camps. Other students and their families find that the summer is an opportunity to do something different that can be added to your résumé. There needs to be a way to do both, to have fun and to engage in challenging activities. Some colleges place a heavy emphasis on summer experiences and others do not.

Working during the year or during the summer is a good way to earn money for college, to get your feet wet in the "real world," and to build vital life skills such as working with others. Colleges typically view work experience positively as long as it doesn't interfere in your school work and your grades don't drop as a result.

If you love to go to camp or to travel during the summer, go to camp or travel the summer after ninth grade and possibly after tenth grade. It would be wise to plan for the summer after eleventh grade for a challenging summer experience. Many parents think a challenging summer experience costs a lot of money, such as a pre-college academic program, which many colleges offer. These programs can cost several thousand dollars. They are not always viewed so positively because they can be expensive, so it is unfair to those who cannot afford to participate. Ask yourself, *What are some worthwhile summer opportunities and how much do they cost?* There are many opportunities available and many of them are totally free! Talk to your guidance counselor, family members, and friends to brainstorm for worthwhile summer experiences.

> **TIP:** Having a part-time job while in high school can be a wonderful experience that is valued by colleges, as long as it doesn't negatively impact your grades. Challenging summer experiences don't have to cost a lot of money.

Our Admissions Counselors on Summer Activities

"Summer activities such as internships or jobs are a great way to develop an interest, build your résumé and earn some money. Remember to take some personal time to relax and have fun, too!"–Cheryl Brown, Director of Undergraduate Admission, Binghamton University, State University of New York

"We find that the students who are going to be most successful at a big school like Indiana University are going to be highly involved in their high school and community throughout the year. Indiana University offers a number of summer programs for high school students who want to explore all that IU has to offer. Some programs include the Young Women's Institute and the Junior Executive Institute in the Kelley School of Business, the High School Journalism Institute, and the Midsummer Theatre Program. Students who are involved in one of our summer programs will stay in the residence halls, meet other prospective students, and experience what life is like at IU."–Lauren Kay, Assistant Director, Indiana University

"Summer activities can help round out a student's academic résumé. For example, study abroad or travel abroad can help demonstrate the student's interests in areas beyond the U.S. Research can be a terrific way to practically apply what has been learned in the class-room and advance a student's knowledge of a particular area beyond what their high school can provide. Volunteer work shows compassion and strong core values, which can help build up a campus community. Even a summer job at the grocery store can show industry and determination, even entrepreneurship. The important thing is to highlight the intrinsic value of what a student did during the summer, and how it relates to the interests of the university to which they are applying."–Raymond Lutzky, Director of Outreach, Rensselaer Polytechnic Institute

"Summer activities are important in developing a total picture of the applicant; activities may include employment during the summer or other times of the year."–Nancy Maly, Director of Admission, Grinnell College

"Summer activities are nice and [pre-college programs] are often money makers for colleges. But here's the question for the applicant. What did you learn about yourself? Why did you participate in such a program? How did others benefit from being in your company? What do you have to offer now that you completed stated program? Sometimes, it's nice for applicants to go to summer camp and enjoy being a teenager."–Mitchell Thompson, Dean of Students, Scarsdale High School, Former Associate Dean of Admissions and Records, The Cooper Union

An internship (usually unpaid for high school students) is a great way to learn about a field of interest. Paid internships and formal internships are very hard to come by for high school students. You may want to investigate an informal internship, set up by contacting people you or family members know, or people in your local community. If you are interested in interior design, for example, call a local interior designer and ask if you can shadow him or her for a month or even during the school year. If you are interested in becoming a teacher, ask if you can work in an after-school program or become a mother's helper during the summer. I know of one resourceful young man who ran into a famous clothing designer while on vacation. He recognized the designer and said he was a big fan of hers. He then proceeded to draw and send her his designs and sent a bouquet of flowers to her room. The next day, she offered him a summer internship! He was definitely in the right place at the right time, but once the opportunity presented itself to him, he recognized it and grabbed it. The possibilities are endless!

Here are a few places you can volunteer in the summer (or during the year):

- Volunteer in a local hospital
- Volunteer in an animal shelter
- Work in a soup kitchen
- Volunteer in a library reading program
- Assist a teacher who is teaching English as a Second Language
- Volunteer for Habitat for Humanity
- Assist in environmental cleanups and/or park beautification programs
- Visit the elderly in nursing homes
- Work with special needs children
- Become a Big Brother/Big Sister
- Shadow an engineer, architect, or doctor

You can check national or local Web sites for internships or places to volunteer. A Better Community, www.abettercommunity.com, sponsored by ABC and "Extreme Home Makeover" is one national Web site to look for opportunities. Other Web sites include www.thevolunteerfamily.org and the federal government's www.studentjobs.gov. It is suggested that you devote at least one summer during high school to a challenging experience of your choice. These opportunities can also provide you with an interesting college essay.

The following Web sites, rated by a high school junior (☺–☺ ☺ ☺ ☺), can be used to find jobs:

Groovejob.com
☺ ☺ ☺
- Job search by locations
- Job search, internship search, volunteer search
- Contains an FAQ section
- Easy to navigate

Teens4hire.org
☺ ☺ ☺
- Create a free membership
- Search jobs
- Apply online
- Contains an About Us section
- Offers a blog spot
- Contains helpful articles (tips for writing a résumé, qualities employers want)

Gotajob.com
☺ ☺ ☺ ☺
- Contains helpful articles
- Offers tips and advice on getting a job
- Teaches how to write a cover letter
- Provides a list of some employers

How important are letters of recommendation?

Letters of recommendation from counselors, teachers, and outside people are subjective factors, that can add weight to your application. Some colleges ask for one teacher or counselor letter, others ask for two teacher letters and a counselor letter, and others don't specify an amount. If you have additional letters from another teacher or an outside person, such as a coach, an internship supervisor, an employer, or someone else, you can include these letters if you and your guidance counselor feel that these letters reveal something about you that is different from your other letters. Colleges do not appreciate receiving four or more letters, unless the letters add significant value to your application. If you have a letter from a senator or a political candidate in whose office you volunteered, but you did not have a personal relationship with that person, the letter is usually filled with fluff and does not reveal anything meaningful about you. After three or four recommendations, most letters become repetitive, so when in doubt, leave it out!

On Letters of Recommendation . . .

"Letters of recommendation serve an important role in the admissions process, because they allow the Admissions Committee to learn more about you from adults who know you well. Choose people who can write about your talents, character and academic skills. People to consider asking include teachers, employers, coaches and community leaders. Don't ask family members to write your letters; for obvious reasons, their comments aren't as credible."–Cheryl Brown, Director of Undergraduate Admissions, Binghamton University, State University of New York

"Rensselaer requires one recommendation letter, preferably from a math or science teacher. A strong recommendation can help confirm that a student is prepared for RPI and will do well. Usually, a math or science teacher will provide a sincere assessment of the student's abilities, good or bad. A half-hearted or weak recommendation usually has little-to-no impact. A recommendation which denounces the student's abilities, however, will kill an application (this is becoming more common as students do not take the time/effort required to find good recommenders). Recommenders should be given two things: respect (their time, their effort, their word, etc.) and information (provide a timeline, addressed envelopes, support material such as a résumé, etc.)."–Raymond Lutzky, Director of Outreach, Rensselaer Polytechnic Institute

Many students wonder which teachers they should ask for letters. Some students incorrectly believe that a teacher in whose class they received an 'A' or high 90s grade is the obvious choice. A class in which you excel could be the right teacher to ask, but a better indicator of your college potential may come from a subject or class where you struggled to do well and made an impression on the teacher with your persistence and motivation to improve. If you have formed a bond with a teacher, that teacher can write more knowledgeably about you than a teacher who barely knows you. If you are an active participant in a class, express interest in a subject, or regularly attend extra help sessions, a teacher can write a more detailed letter about you, which is what college counselors want to read.

College admissions counselors don't want to read general letters that read, "Tim is a quiet and studious student who gets 100s on all my tests." They would rather read letters that are specific, such as "Tim is an intellectually curious student who stayed after class to engage me in conversation about a book he recently read for pleasure. He does not have the highest average in the class, but he does have a passion for learning, and his paper on the use of herbal medicines in Chinatown was carefully researched, well organized, and featured critical analyses of primary and secondary sources." Which letter would you rather read: One that is

> **TIP:** Choose carefully which teachers to ask for letters of recommendation. Ask teachers who know you well, not necessarily whose classes in which you performed the best.

general and says very little about the person or one that is specific and says a great deal about the person's academic potential in college? So, the bottom line is to choose carefully who to ask for letters of recommendation.

Now that you have an idea about who to ask, when is the best time to ask a teacher to write a letter for you? You can ask teachers during your junior year (or earlier) if they will write a letter of recommendation. Some teachers write letters over the summer, so make sure you ask them before the end of your junior year, and then remind them at the beginning of your senior year. Can teachers say no when you ask them to write a letter? Absolutely! It is their right to decline to write a letter if they don't feel they can write an effective letter for you. My husband, a physics teacher, has on occasion turned down students, but he is usually very tactful about how he does it. He usually says, "I think it's a good idea if you ask another teacher." If a teacher hems and haws and doesn't say yes right away, it may be an indication that he or she cannot write a terrific letter for you. Many teachers do not want to hurt a student's feelings, so they write a lukewarm letter which does not really help your case. When you ask teachers, you could say, "Do you feel comfortable writing a letter of recommendation for me?" or "Do you think you can write a strong letter of recommendation for me?" If they say yes, that's great. If they hesitate or say no, then you probably should ask a different teacher.

The best letters are from teachers who know you well, who you have formed a bond with, and in whose class you have either performed fairly well or demonstrated interest. Guidance counselor letters are usually required—another good reason to get to know your counselor. A specific letter from a teacher, counselor, or outside person can enhance your college application, and can demonstrate what type of student and person you are and your readiness for college.

> **TIP:** One way to ask a teacher to write you a letter is to say, "Do you feel comfortable writing a letter for me" or "Do you think you can write a strong letter of recommendation for me?"

Is an interview required?

Many students dread a personal interview, but it is a valuable opportunity for you to find out more information about a college and to plead your case as to why you should be admitted. Some colleges require interviews, some say an interview is optional, and others do not interview at all. Information about whether colleges offer interviews can be found on college Web sites. An interview may be conducted by an admissions officer, an alumnus of the college, or a student.

If you are given an opportunity to have an interview, you should accept, as it is a good way to exchange information. For some colleges, you are responsible for contacting the admissions office to set up an interview on or off campus; others may call you to schedule an interview. An on-campus interview can be scheduled for the same day as a campus tour. Off-campus interviews are usually held in your hometown, and are conducted by an alumnus in your area. One of the most common places to meet is at a Starbuck's or other coffee establishment. The interview typically lasts 20–60 minutes or longer. The interview is not usually a critical factor in the application process, unless you are applying for a special program, such as a very competitive combined B.A./M.D. or similar program, a learning disability program, or an honors program. Most interviewers write a summary of the interview, noting their impressions of your academic accomplishments, extracurricular activities, personal characteristics, and anticipated fit in their college. After the interview, interviewers sometimes assign a numerical score or rank for the admissions committee to take into account when they review your application.

If you are applying to an art school, a portfolio review may be required or it may be optional. If you have the ability to attend a portfolio review in person, it is a valuable way to meet potential admissions officers or art professors, convey your interest, and obtain feedback about your work, sometimes before you officially submit the portfolio. More information about special talent portfolios is contained in Chapter 6.

How do I best prepare for an interview?

Do not become overly distressed before the interview, as the interview can help you but rarely hurt you. You can prepare for the interview by doing the following:

- Do some soul searching
- Assess your personality
- Consider your strengths and weaknesses
- Assess your academic experience—be familiar with your transcript
- Evaluate your outside interests and activities
- Examine your values and goals
- Clarify what's important to you and what you are looking for in a college
- Try to anticipate some interview questions
- Research the college's Web site

Some possible interview questions are:

- What career/major are you interested in?
- Tell me about yourself.
- What are your strengths and weaknesses?
- What books have your read? What are you reading now?
- Who do you most admire and why?
- What is your favorite subject?

- What do you do for fun or in your spare time?
- In which extracurricular activities have you participated?
- What leadership skills do you possess?
- Why do you want to attend this college? What impact will you have on campus?
- Where do you see yourself in 5 years, 10 years?
- If you could meet any past or present historical or fictional figure, who would you like to meet?
- What challenges have you faced?
- What have you done during the summer?
- What is a national or local issue that concerns you?

During the interview, you should, as silly as it sounds, try to relax and to be yourself. Some tips for how to conduct yourself during the interview include:

- Be prepared and be polite
- Be prompt
- Dress appropriately
- Don't appear over-rehearsed
- Listen to the interviewer
- Maintain eye contact—this is critical!
- Try to avoid one-word answers
- Show your interest in the interviewer and try to make a connection. Ask about their experiences during college and ask what they are doing now
- Demonstrate your interest and knowledge about the college
- Ask probing questions, which are not thoroughly covered in the course catalog or Web site, about the college

Here are some things you should *not* do during the interview:

- Don't ask the interviewer to compare colleges.
- Don't make excuses for poor SAT/ACT scores, grades, or why a teacher dislikes you.
- Don't give academic information (transcript, SAT/ACT scores) unless someone asks or it.
- Don't ask obvious questions, such as how many students does this college have or do you have an education program or physical therapy major? You should already know the answers to these basic questions.

At the end of the interview, thank the interviewer and ask for his address or e-mail address so you can write a thank you note, and do so promptly. If you have follow-up questions, you have a person to contact there for additional information. Even if an interview doesn't carry significant weight, you should always try to make a good impression and to be enthusiastic.

What role does technology play in the application process?

As technology plays an increasingly important role in the application process, there are some issues that you need to be aware of and that could negatively impact you. Almost every college requires a student's e-mail address and sometimes the parents' e-mail address. Some students have old addresses from when they were in middle school that are no longer appropriate. Take an objective look at your e-mail address; if it says sexymama@aol.com, ihateschool@aol.com, or something like partyanimal@aol.com, I would strongly suggest that you change your e-mail address to something neutral. Students also don't realize that colleges can and sometimes do access Facebook and MySpace profiles.

If you would be embarrassed by anything posted on these Web sites, be very careful what you post during the college application process. For that matter, high schools and employers can also look at postings, so be very mindful of what's on your profile. Photos of drinking binges, risqué photos, rumors about others, and other inappropriate behavior can be the kiss of death for some colleges and honors programs. Also, be vigilant about passwords and giving people you hardly know access to your accounts, as some students hack into other people's profiles and try to sabotage their college acceptances by posting harmful photos. Do you really have 600 close friends on Facebook? Take a look at your profile and delete anyone you're not 100 percent sure about. In the beginning of your senior year, take a look at your e-mail address and your online postings. You should change the security access to your account and delete any inappropriate material.

On the positive side, technology has made applying to college somewhat easier and more accessible. The Common Application and the Universal College Application are two of the most popular ways to apply to college. An emerging trend is to develop electronic or e-portfolios, which colleges can review to provide them with even more information about your talents, skills, and abilities. These portfolios can contain creative works, images, links, research papers, and other documents highlighting your various accomplishments. If you're careful, technology can be very useful during the college admissions process. If you're not careful, you may inadvertently give negative information to colleges, which can be used to reject your application.

Other sources for obtaining students' perspectives of college life include blogs, videos, and chat rooms which can be accessed on a college's Web site. You have the opportunity to talk to current students about academic and campus life. Talking directly to students can offer new insights into a potential college.

How You Should Judge Colleges: What Students Should Look For

Private universities offer more courses and smaller classes than do public universities.

State universities are a much better value; save your money for graduate school.

The hot school this year is _____; you should apply there!

I've never heard of that college; you should apply to a "name" college.

Everyone has an opinion on where you should go to college, from your Aunt Debbie to your mother's hairdresser to your father's accountant. Who do you listen to and where do you get reliable information about potential colleges?

What are my sources of information about colleges?

There are many sources of information about colleges, and very few are neutral or objective. Colleges try to get your attention with glossy brochures, cool Web sites, enticing letters, and free stuff (T-shirts, pens, and other freebies). Parents, family members, and friends sometimes have their own agenda, such as convincing you to attend a university with a known name or to go to a college they attended. Many students and parents are swayed by college guides and college rankings (published ratings of colleges), of which there are many.

The following sources can be used to obtain information about colleges:

- **Family Members:** Family members have a wealth of knowledge and opinions on the subject of where you should go to college. Aunts, uncles, cousins, and other relatives come out of the woodwork to offer unsolicited advice. Their advice may be based on personal experiences, rumors, and what they've read or heard in the media. Some advice may be legitimate, some may not. Remember, what is best for one relative may not be best for you. You should absolutely listen to your parents, as they know you better than anyone. You should also have a frank discussion with your parents regarding how much they can afford to pay for college as well as other parameters they want you to consider while conducting your college search.

> ## Helicopter Parents
>
> Parents can and should offer assistance during the college admissions process, but, again, too much assistance is not wise either. The term "helicopter parent" has been coined to refer to parents who are too involved in the college admissions process, from writing essays to excessively calling guidance counselors to talking nonstop on campus visits to tour guides and admissions counselors. This term can carry over into the student's first year, referring to parents who call too much, give too much advice, and create too much dependency on the part of the student.

- **Guidance Counselors:** Your high school guidance counselor can be a valuable ally and resource during the process. Guidance counselors can direct you to legitimate sources or information and may also have vital information you may not have access to, so definitely try to pick his or her brain. Keep in mind that many counselors have caseloads of 250+ students, so sometimes their time is limited. Most students meet with their counselor and one or both parents in the spring of their junior year, in meetings that generally last one to two periods. Check the resources available in your counselor's office for postings about open houses, visits from college representatives, scholarships, financial aid, and other information.

- **Teachers:** Teachers can be a wonderful resource for information about colleges. Always ask your teachers where they went to school, as you may find an alumnus from a college you are interested in attending. They may tell you about a college you never heard of that might be a viable option for you.

- **Friends/Peers:** Friends and peers are another important source of information for you. Sharing information you have gained about colleges is of benefit to everyone. Siblings of your friends may currently be attending a school you are interested in, and you could attend classes with them when you make a campus visit. Again, some of the information you hear may not be 100 percent accurate, so keep that in mind.

- **College Web Sites:** College Web sites are an invaluable tool for gathering information about colleges you are considering. On a college Web site, you can view the campus, look at dorm rooms, examine the curriculum of academic programs, look at scholarships, costs, and financial aid information, and see what clubs and activities are offered. You can also check into core requirements or general education requirements you have to take once you enroll in college. Many students neglect to check these requirements and then they are surprised when they have to take foreign language classes, a physical education class, math, or another subject they didn't want to take in college. Some colleges are very loose on required courses and others have heavy-duty core requirements.

A great search tool to use on a college's Web site is its "Common Data Set," which gives you access to a wide range of information, including what factors they use in admissions, what majors students apply to, how many students are offered waitlist positions, and much other useful data. To obtain the information contained in this important tool, search for "Common Data Set" in the college's search field. A more streamlined place to access important admissions information is the "Freshman Profile" or "Entering Class Profile." Here you find the average GPA for accepted students, the middle 50 percent of SAT/ACT scores, the number of students who were admitted, and other useful information. A college's Web site is the first place to look for specific information about a college, followed by a campus tour.

In addition to college Web sites, there are many networking Web sites that offer information about colleges. As long as you are aware that not all of the information is accurate or has been checked by independent people, some of the information may be useful. In addition to the College Board and Princeton Review, there are matchmaking sites similar in concept to online dating. You can search by location, major, size, cost, and other factors. Some sites are produced by students, and the information is uncut and unfiltered. You can use these sites in your initial information-gathering period.

A high school junior has identified the following two Web sites, along with their features, as the most valuable for students:

www.collegeconfidential.com ☺ ☺ ☺ ☺

- ❏ Financial aid calculator
- ❏ Ask the dean section
- ❏ Articles
- ❏ College search by location, name, or area of study
- ❏ College rankings links

www.mycollegeoptions.org ☺ ☺ ☺ ☺

- ❏ College search by city/state, name, or major
- ❏ Research a major
- ❏ Free profile includes college match report and a monthly newsletter

---

🎓 **Campus Visits:** Taking a tour of campus is one of the best ways to determine which college is right for you. If at all possible, visit campuses before you apply. Chapter 4 is devoted exclusively to campus visits and how to make the most out of your trip.

College Fairs: College fairs are a fun and easy way to explore many different colleges at one time. Some are sponsored by the National Association of College Admissions Counselors (NACAC), others by regional counseling groups, consortiums of several high schools in your area, or college fairs conducted by your own high school. College fairs can open your eyes to colleges you might not have previously considered, so keep an open mind at these fairs. You can talk to college representatives, put your name on a mailing list, and obtain phone numbers and e-mails from college representatives to ask futher questions. One tip is to bring preprinted mailing labels with your name, address, and e-mail address, so you don't have to fill out individual requests for more information. It is never too early to attend college fairs, as they give you access to many colleges in one shot—and it's a good way to obtain freebies (pens, mugs, banners) and promotional materials from colleges.

College Guides: There are many college guides on the market. Some guides are written by the College Board, Princeton Review, Peterson's, Kaplan, and other companies, and some are distributed by independent counselors and professional writers. The information in these books is based on input from surveys of college admissions directors or college students, or from objective or subjective research. My personal favorites are *Fiske's Guide to Colleges* (Sourcebooks, Inc., 2008) and *Rugg's Recommendations on The Colleges* (Rugg's Recommendations, 2008). Rugg's enables you to search for colleges by major. College guide books can assist you in looking at basic information, such as size, location, cost, deadlines, and what majors are offered. They can be very useful, but don't base your impressions about colleges solely on these books.

College Rankings: As long as you don't take them too seriously and you read everything carefully, college rankings can be another source of information about colleges. The most famous college rankings list is published yearly in late summer by *US News & World Report.* Other published rankings include *Kiplingers, Forbes,* and *Business Week.* College rankings can be helpful, but they can also be misleading. Parents are generally impressed and rely heavily on these rankings, whereas guidance counselors are usually not so impressed because some of the indicators used to determine the rankings can be manipulated. Many colleges like to see their ranking position move up each year, so they spend a lot of time and money to ensure that their college is highly ranked. Other colleges have decided not to participate in the survey which is used to determine the rankings, because some of the indicators used to compose the rankings are based on how much money alumni give, SAT/ACT scores, and other factors which can be manipulated. A well-regarded book on the subject of rankings (or antirankings) is *College Unranked: Ending the College Admissions Frenzy* (Harvard University Press, 2005), edited by Lloyd Thacker of the Education Conservancy.

Visits by College Representatives: Some high schools invite admissions counselors from colleges that are popular with their students to visit the high school. You usually need to sign up in advance to attend these sessions, which are very beneficial. You can sometimes meet the person who will be reading your application, so it is a good idea to introduce yourself after the session and let the person know you are interested in their college. You can ask questions in an informal setting and get their contact information, so you can keep in touch with them during the application process. Many admissions counselors do in fact remember students they have met in visits to high schools, so definitely take advantage of this important opportunity.

> **Tip:** The information overload during the college admissions process can be overwhelming at times. There is a lot of information out there, but not all of it is accurate. It is your job to research and carefully consider all sources of information during your college search.

- 🎓 **College Mailings:** You may be receiving mail from colleges you have never heard of and are wondering where all of the mail from various colleges is coming from. If you answered "yes" on the PSAT, SAT, or ACT registration forms or answer sheets to receive mailings, this is why you are getting all this mail. If you haven't yet filled out the registration forms or boxes, and don't want to be inundated with mail, simply check "no."

- 🎓 **Previous Graduates from Your High School:** Previous graduates of your high school often have "the real dirt" about college campuses, as long as you trust the source of the information. Many high schools invite graduates back during winter break to share stories and experiences about their freshman year, which can be very helpful to you. If your high school does not do this, you should ask them to do so.

What factors should I consider in evaluating colleges?

There are many factors to consider when evaluating prospective colleges. It is up to you and your family to determine which criteria is most relevant for you. Some criteria are "make or break" ones, things that the colleges on your list must have in order for you to consider them; others would be desirable to have but they are not mandatory. If you can identify your "must haves" and optional factors ahead of time, making a decision as to which college to attend might be a little easier for you.

The following criteria should be taken into account when assessing possible colleges; only you know how much weight to give each one. Thinking about each factor carefully helps you shorten your list of potential colleges where you feel the most comfortable.

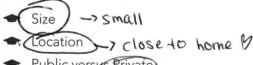

- 🎓 (Size) → small
- 🎓 (Location) → close to home ♡
- 🎓 Public versus (Private)
- 🎓 Academic Programs
- 🎓 Student Diversity
- 🎓 Male/Female Ratio
- 🎓 Campus Life
- 🎓 Athletics

- Cost
- Admissions Standards/Selectivity
- Facilities/Technology
- Family Issues
- Disability Services
- Study Abroad Programs/Co-ops/Internships

Let's take a look at each of these factors.

Size

Colleges come in many sizes, typically ranging from 1,000 students (a small college) to over 30,000 students (an extra large college). There are pros and cons of attending a small versus a large college. The size of the college may affect the number and selection of courses offered, opportunities for getting to know professors and students, the diversity of the students, and the types of campus activities that are offered. Our daughter attended a medium-sized private university which she loved, but it didn't offer as many course selections as much larger universities.

If you come from a small high school, going to a supersized university may be overwhelming for you. Conversely, if you attend a large high school, going to a small university may feel stifling. Generally speaking, a smaller college has fewer courses to offer and there may be fewer clubs and campus activities to choose from. On the other hand, a smaller college may have smaller classes, making it easier to get to know professors and students. A larger college tends to have more courses to choose from, a more diverse student body, and more athletic teams and campus activities.

If you are unsure about your college major, a larger college usually offers more majors. If you switch majors, a bigger school is more likely to offer your new major, so you wouldn't have to transfer to another school. One of the best ways to decide what size college is best for you is to visit small, moderately sized, and large schools to get a feel for which type of school fits best.

Location

Location refers to both how far you are from home and whether you attend college in a rural town, a suburb, or a city. Location is a factor in which your family members may have strong opinions. Many students prefer to apply to colleges within two to four hours from their home, which gives students the flexibility of coming home between vacations. Many parents usually feel most comfortable with this distance from home. There are many questions you need to ask yourself when considering location as a factor in choosing a college:

- In what part of the country would you like to live during college?
- Do you prefer to attend college in a city, suburb, small town, or rural area?
- How close would you like to be to your home and your family?

- Can you afford airfare or train fare if you attend a college far from home?
- Can you and/or your family afford out-of-state tuition if you choose to attend college in another state? (This is discussed further in Chapter 7.)

The answers to these questions depend on how independent you are, your family situation, your finances, and your preferences for different types of climate. If one of your hobbies is skiing, then a cold climate would make sense for you. If, however you are a surfer, then a warmer climate would be best if you want to pursue your hobby. If you have a family member who is ill, you may need to be closer to home. If you want to become more independent and live away from home, then living at a college a few hours from home might be ideal.

PUBLIC VERSUS PRIVATE

There are definite differences in attending a public versus private institution. A public university is state funded and usually has lower tuition than a private university. A private university is privately funded, and usually has higher tuition than a public university. If you are a resident of a state, you save money by attending a school in your state's university system. If you are out of state, prepare to spend more money on tuition; however, it usually costs less money than a private university. One of the biggest bargains is the State University of New York (SUNY) system, which currently does not charge significantly more for out of state residents. When a friend's son in a neighboring state was looking for a quality but reasonably priced university, I steered his family toward the SUNY system. Other bargains can be found on Kiplinger's list of "100 Best Values in Public Colleges" available at Kiplinger.com. Private universities generally cost more than public universities, but with scholarships and financial aid, that may not always be the case. Many private universities have endowments, and they use these funds to attract students who are academically gifted or who will add to the diversity of their student population. It would be wise to compare the total costs of all colleges you are considering after you receive a financial aid package. More information about financial aid and scholarships is found in Chapter 7.

In addition to the financial aspect, there are other differences between a private and a public university. In times of economic distress, public universities may suffer from budget cuts from their state's legislature, which could translate into fewer course offerings or larger classes. Private universities are not immune to budget cuts in economic downturns, but they may have more endowments to cover difficult times. Private universities sometimes offer more perks in terms of course offerings, food choices, dorm rooms, smaller class sizes, and more expansive celebrations. Open house receptions may be more lavish in private colleges, but that is a superficial perk which doesn't affect the academic reputation of a university. Some parents believe a private university is superior academically to a public university, but that is simply not the case especially for the "Public Ivies." Richard Moll created the term "Public Ivy" (Viking Penguin, Inc., 1985) to refer to public universities which offer an Ivy League quality education at a public university for a deeply discounted price. Moll's original list of eight public universities has been expanded by Greene's Guides (Collins, 2001) and others to include additional Public Ivies.

Some Public Ivies

Binghamton University, State University of New York (NY)

College of William and Mary (VA)

Indiana University–Bloomington (IN)

Miami University (OH)

Rutgers University–New Brunswick, The State University of New Jersey (NJ)

University of California (CA)

University of Colorado–Boulder (CO)

University of Florida–Gainesville (FL)

University of Maryland–College Park (MD)

University of Michigan–Ann Arbor (MI)

University of North Carolina–Chapel Hill (NC)

University of Texas–Austin (TX)

University of Vermont (VT)

University of Virginia (VA)

University of Wisconsin–Madison (WI)

ACADEMIC PROGRAMS

The areas of study or majors offered by a college influence your decision to attend a college or university. Although the terms *college* and *university* are usually used interchangeably, there are some differences between them. A college is typically a smaller school which offers various degree programs within one college. They offer degrees at the bachelor's level, and some also offer degrees at the master's degree level. A university has several colleges within the broader university that offer specialized programs of study, such as a College or School of Education, Engineering, Nursing, or Business. A university offers more degree programs as well as doctoral level programs, including J.D. (Juris Doctor) and PhD (Doctor of Philosophy).

A majority of students enter college unsure of their major or area of study. It is very common not to know what your future career will be at the age of 17 or 18. One of the goals of attending college is to explore different subject areas, and many colleges encourage exploration during the first two years of school through what they call a *core curriculum*—a series of courses designed to introduce you to courses in the arts, literature, social sciences, math and sciences, and other areas. Typically, you do not have to declare your major until the end of your sophomore or the beginning of your junior year. It is also not unusual to change your major one or more times. So, how do you take into account academic programs when selecting a college?

Most liberal arts colleges offer psychology, history, math, English, and other common majors. If you are thinking about education, engineering, or business programs, you may want to look at a university where more programs of study are offered. Within the university, they may have separate colleges for different areas of professional study, such as a School of Education, a School of Business, or a School of Engineering. If you are considering a very specific major, such as linguistics, creative writing, broadcasting, physical therapy, or speech pathology, you have to check the list of majors offered at each university to ensure they offer your potential area of study.

Keep in mind that if you are considering going into the medical or legal profession, there is no pre-med or pre-law major in college. Rather, you select pre-law or pre-med as an advisement option. What this means is that you can major in any program of study, as long as you take the required prerequisites to enter a professional program or graduate school. You will be offered an advisor throughout your college years, who helps prepare you for these professional programs after you complete your undergraduate degree.

STUDENT DIVERSITY

Colleges vary widely in the diversity of their college population. Most colleges offer a breakdown of their student population by geographic location and by student diversity. These statistics can be found in the college's view book (marketing materials sent to students or found in high school guidance offices), on its Web site, or in college guides, which can be found in any public library.

If you are looking for low student diversity and you want to attend college with students similar to you, then you might be interested in a Historically Black college, a religious-affiliated university (Roman Catholic, Methodist, Baptist, etc.), or a women's college or men's college.

If you are looking for high student diversity, a larger college or university would tend to have more student diversity, drawing from all areas of the United States and other countries. Some students feel more comfortable living and learning in an environment with others who are like them. Other students prefer to interact with and meet people from a variety of racial, ethnic, and cultural groups.

MALE/FEMALE RATIO

The male/female ratio on university campuses has changed to the point where it has become a factor to consider when researching potential colleges. Colleges which have very imbalanced female to male ratios greater than the norm of 60 percent females versus 40 percent males may be in jeopardy of losing students. When our youngest daughter was looking for colleges, she expressed concern over this ratio and it did play a role in choosing which college to attend. She didn't want to attend a school where the female to male ratio was too lopsided. On the other hand, when a friend's son heard about the ratio issue, he wanted to apply to schools which had many more females, so it all depends on your perspective!

There are some colleges that work very hard to balance the male/female ratio. This policy, however, can backfire when recruiting students, as it is possible that some well-qualified girls could be rejected in order to attract more boys in order to maintain a gender balance. Other engineering and technical schools, such as Massachusetts Institute of Technology (MIT), Rensselaer Polytechnic Institute (RPI), California Institute of Technology (Cal Tech), and Harvey Mudd, struggle to attract more female students, so girls may have a slight advantage in applying to these specialty schools.

If the male/female ratio concerns you, then you should be aware of the ratio at a prospective college. The information about the gender ratio is usually available on a college's Web site under the "Freshman Profile" or "Class Profile" of the entering class.

CAMPUS LIFE

Campus life can be defined as organized activities or spontaneous events that exist on or off campus. On most campuses, depending on your personality and interests, you can find an activity that you enjoy. Some campuses offer a Greek life, with sororities and fraternities, and your social life is often built around your adopted "brothers" and "sisters."

Many colleges offer a variety of activities, including student government, campus media (newspapers, magazines, and radio stations), honor societies, academic clubs (Anthropology Club, Psychology Club), community service/ social action clubs (Circle K, Students Against Destructive Decisions), special interest groups (a cappella singing groups, anime, photography), cultural organizations (Asian Student Association, Latino Students United, African Peoples Organization), and religious organizations (Hillel, Muslim Student Association).

> **TIP:** Don't give too much weight to labels, such as "party school," "nerdy school," "preppy school," etc. Many parents are concerned about their child attending a "party school." Although there are published lists of "party schools," realistically any school can be a party school if that's what you're looking for, so don't give much weight to any kind of label.

A school's geographic location, academic reputation, and whether or not it is a commuter college (where most students go home on weekends) can all affect student social life. As an incoming freshman, you want to get a feel for a college's campus life before you enroll. If you were involved in a club in high school, you may want to continue your involvement with that organization or look for new experiences. As a freshman, it's very important to immediately get involved in campus life as a way to make friends, avoid being homesick, and fully participate in college life.

ATHLETICS

Athletics is an important issue to consider if you play sports competitively or if you enjoy watching or playing sports for fun. If you play competitively, you may be eligible to participate in the National Collegiate Athletic Association (NCAA), which determines the rules regarding eligibility, recruiting, and financial aid for athletes. Students who intend to play a sport in college may want a Division I or II college, and students must be certified by the NCAA eligibility center. There are minimum grades, standardized test scores, and courses required for athletes. For more information, go to www.ncaa.org.

COST

Cost, of course, is an important consideration in deciding which college to attend. You are not alone if you and your family are already worried about the cost of college, which has been steadily increasing. The cost of attending college includes:

- Tuition
- Fees (activity, registration, lab, and gym fees)
- Room and Board (housing and meal plan)
- Books and supplies
- Personal expenses (entertainment, laundry, . . .)

- ☍ Transportation (expenses to and from home, whether commuting or living on campus)
- ☍ Miscellaneous expenses (sports, fraternity/sorority, . . .)

Many students are hesitant to discuss the price tag of college when they are researching colleges. This issue is too important to discuss later on, after you've fallen in love with a school out of your price range. Don't be afraid to discuss the financial reality of your situation during the initial stages of the college application process. Then when you receive your financial aid packages, you can freely discuss which college suits you best and is financially affordable. Information about financial aid is discussed in Chapter 7.

ADMISSIONS STANDARDS/SELECTIVITY

How selective or competitive a college or university is can help you to decide if it is the right college for you. Later in the chapter, I'll discuss how it is appropriate for you to choose a mix of schools, based upon your qualifications for admission. Colleges are generally categorized as less competitive, competitive, highly competitive, or most competitive. When selecting a prospective school, you need to examine what your qualifications (grades, difficulty of high school courses, and SAT/ACT scores) are, as compared to a college's admissions standards. The more selective or competitive the college, the harder it will be for you to gain acceptance.

FACILITIES/TECHNOLOGY

When evaluating potential colleges, you should explore, through research and visits, the college's facilities. Facilities may include things like the athletic teams and fields, the library, the dorms, the food, the physical buildings and classrooms, the safety and security of the campus, and the use of state-of-the-art technology. All of these aspects of a campus's facilities add to or enhance your experience at a particular college.

If you are considering a college for its athletic programs or for special talent (art, drama, dance, etc.), then its athletic fields or performance halls should be of vital interest to you. The dorms you will be living in during your college years can also affect your overall happiness there. Most freshman dorms are small, but as you become an upperclassman, your choice of housing improves. Campus food consists of several dining options, depending on what's offered by that college. If you have dietary restrictions, such as vegetarian, kosher, or halal, you should make sure the college offers what you need. You need to select a meal plan (usually based on two or three meals a day for five to seven days per week) if you live on campus. You may hear people talking about the "freshman 15," which refers to some freshmen who gain weight during their first year because of unlimited access to food which is hard to resist.

The physical buildings and classroom facilities can add to a college's beauty and attraction. When considering a college, you may want to think about how far you have to walk from a parking lot or your dorm to get to the majority of your classes, and whether the physical appearance of the college appeals to you. Some colleges feature beautiful, older architecture, while others feature a sleek, more modern style. Is a college campus undergoing construction or renovations? If so, can you live with the noise and inconvenience during the construction?

Safety and security on campuses have become more essential in recent years. On most college tours, a guide discusses what the college does to maintain a safe and secure environment, including emergency phones, escort services at night, security guards or a

> **TIP:** Always ask colleges about their campus security measures so parents feel comfortable in sending you there.

police force, locked dorms, and other measures. Colleges do not readily disclose their crime statistics, but this is an important question to ask about as you are screening potential schools. Many colleges have set up instant communication methods with students via cell phones and text messaging to alert you to security situations on campus so you can take swift action if necessary.

The growing use of state-of-the-art technology is in evidence at many colleges. You want to know which colleges use wireless technology, have internet access in their dorms and class-rooms, and which offer free computers or discounted rentals or purchase plans. Many colleges are using "smart boards" in their classroom for instruction, where professors can display Pow-erPoint presentations and integrate the Internet as necessary. Other uses of technology include Web-based communication programs, such as Blackboard or Moodle, which allow for interaction between students and professors. On a recent visit to the University of California at Berke-ley (Cal), we were impressed that many of the lectures were recorded and available for students to watch from the comfort of their dorm rooms.

FAMILY ISSUES

Family issues, including divorce and illness, can play a role in which colleges you want to consider attending. You may have dreamed of attending school in another part of the coun-try, but if you have a sick mother or grandmother, this plan may not be possible. Consider your family's circumstances and wishes when selecting possible schools in order to avoid conflicts later on.

DISABILITY SERVICES

If you have been receiving support services in high school, you may want to continue receiving services in college. In high school, you may have received extended time on tests, use of a computer for essays, a reader, a listening device, or some other accommodation. These ser-vices, if you have an Individualized Education Plan (IEP) or 504 Plan, were mandated in high school under the Individuals with Disabilities Act (IDEA). Once you are in college, your parent's legal authority has ended, and you must advocate for yourself. Advocating for yourself includes knowing everything about your disability, speaking up for yourself, and making decisions for yourself. Many colleges have resources available for you, although you must find out about these services yourself; no one will contact you.

Before you complete high school, your parents can ask for a close-out meeting, where your family and the professionals you have been working with in high school can discuss what services, if any, you feel you need in college. It is very important that you obtain current (usually within one year) psycho-educational testing (consisting of cognitive and academic achievement tests), which you can provide to colleges. You should also know the name of your specific disability, whether it is Attention Deficit Hyperactivity Disorder (ADHD), a learning disability, a physical disability, or another type of disability. How does the disability impact your learning and your overall life? Will you be able to manage living on campus, or would you be better off commuting to a college?

You do not need to identify yourself as a student with a disability in the admissions process, unless you want to or you are applying to a special program for students with disabilities. Once you are admitted, however, you should make an appointment with the Office of Disability Services (called different offices in various colleges) and sit down with these professionals to discuss your needs in college.

Most colleges offer some type of service. Others offer full programs with higher fees, depending on what type of services you require. There are some colleges that are exclusively for students with disabilities, such as Landmark College in Vermont. Landmark describes itself as a college for high potential students with learning disabilities and ADHD. You may decide you do not need any services in college, and you could function very well on your own. However, you may want to inform your professors so they are aware of your disability. The choice is yours, but you should become educated about your disability before choosing a college.

Some Colleges That Offer Disability Services or Programs

Adelphi University	Manhattanville College
American University	Marist College
Clark University	Mitchell College
Curry College	Muskingum College
Hofstra University	Rochester Institute of Technology
Iona College	St. Thomas Aquinas College, NY
Landmark College	University of Arizona
Lynn University	

STUDY-ABROAD PROGRAMS/CO-OPS/INTERNSHIPS

Two areas in which students are usually very interested are study-abroad programs and internships. Study-abroad programs give students an opportunity to broaden their perspectives, to immerse themselves in other countries while they are still in college, and to earn credits while spending time away from campus.

When researching colleges, you should find out if the university offers study-abroad options. Colleges and tour guides usually indicate what percent of their students participate in study-abroad programs, but you need to get details about these programs before you commit to them. Do students usually get their first-choice program? Do you need to speak the language of the country you want to visit? Is tuition the same as what you would pay on campus? What additional expenses will there be? Will you get course credit or will participating delay your graduation?

Most colleges offer some type of study-abroad program, so make sure you get comprehensive information before you select a college based on the reputation of these programs.

Other colleges are known for their co-operative (co-op) programs. These programs can give you an advantage when you are looking for a job after graduation. Co-op programs give you on-the-job experience while you are still in college. Many colleges provide students with internships either during the school year or during the summer. When visiting colleges, ask about the reputation of the internship office, and whether or not the college has the resources to help you find an appropriate internship.

Study abroad, co-op programs, and internships can provide you with a worthwhile college experience which can enhance your résumé and assist you during your job hunt after college.

Some Colleges That Offer Co-op Programs

Drexel University	Rochester Institute of Technology
Georgia Institute of Technology	University of Cincinnati
Johnson & Wales	University of Louisville
Long Island University	University of Waterloo
Kettering University	Wentworth Institute of Technology
Northeastern University	
Pace University	

How many colleges should be on my list?

It is a good idea to start with a fairly large list of colleges (15–20). Then through campus visits, research, and an evaluation of all of the factors discussed in this chapter, you can whittle down the list to a reasonable amount of colleges to which you can apply. If you are not opposed to living in another part of the country, it is a good idea to "think outside the box" when contemplating prospective colleges.

Some students apply to 3–5 colleges, others apply to as many as 12–15 colleges; many students are somewhere in the middle. If you are an average student considering moderately selective colleges, applying to 3–5 schools is just fine. If you are an above average student and you are considering selective to highly selective colleges, then you may want to apply to a few more schools, with a final list of about 6–8 schools. If you are in the top 10–15 percent of your senior class and you are interested in the most selective schools in the country, you may want to apply to even more schools, settling on between 8–12 (or more) colleges, because of the stiff competition to the most selective colleges.

Application Fees

Application fees can vary from no fee to as high as $75 or more. If there are schools to which you want to apply but your family cannot afford the hefty application fees, talk to your guidance counselor about fee waivers. You can receive fee waivers for taking standardized tests, sending score reports, and applying to college. In some cases, your guidance counselor can write a letter to a college on school stationery requesting a fee waiver. An application fee should not stop you from applying to the college or colleges of your choice.

With the introduction of the Common Application and the Universal Application, students have been known to apply to 15 or more colleges because of the ease of applying using these streamlined applications. However, when you apply to so many schools, it becomes more difficult to establish that you are serious about all of these schools, because you may not have the time to visit all of them before you apply. It is also hard to write detailed essays for each school when you have so many essays to write. In times of economic distress, students tend to apply to more colleges as they do not know how enrollment will be impacted by financial hardships and they do not know if their financial aid packages will be high enough for them to attend the institution of their choice.

Do I need to apply to a range of schools?

It is wise to apply to a range of schools to cover all possibilities and ensure that you have several colleges on your list where you could see yourself happy for four years. In past years, many guidance counselors used the terms *safety, target,* and *reach* schools to describe a range of schools for students. Due to changing economic and demographic conditions, the use of the term *safety school* may no longer be warranted as there are too many unknown variables in the college admissions process. More appropriate terms may be *probable or highly likely* schools (instead of safety), *likely or realistic* schools (instead of target), and *dream, or unlikely* schools (instead of reach).

If you apply to an average of six to nine schools, then it is suggested that you apply to two or three from each category. It is important to make sure that *each* school on your list is one in which you would be not just content but happy. This concept is really vital because some students do end up at a probable or highly likely school and then realize they really don't want to go to that school and become unhappy and disappointed. If you carefully research each choice and take the time to visit, your choices will all be good ones and you will have a more enjoyable freshman year. Many students have their heart set on a reach school, and when they are not accepted, they are devastated. A much healthier attitude is to make sure all of your potential college choices are schools where you can really see yourself.

Whether you apply to 2 or 15 colleges, do not apply to schools that you definitely would not want to attend. If you apply to a college you have absolutely no intention of attending, you could potentially be taking a spot from your peers, which is not fair to them and you could be damaging the reputation of your high school. If a high school has a reputation of students applying to a particular college and no one from your high school actually attends that school for a few years, the college could deny future students based on a pattern of students not attending.

PROBABLE OR HIGHLY LIKELY SCHOOLS

Probable or highly likely schools are typically colleges in which you have a high (90 percent) chance of being accepted. They should be schools in which you can visualize yourself being comfortable and where you believe you can be academically and socially successful. You should check the admissions standards of these colleges and you and your guidance counselor should believe you fall comfortably within their standards.

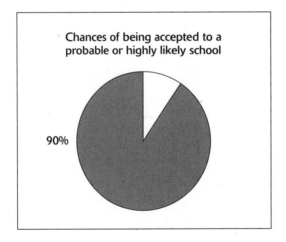

Chances of being accepted to a probable or highly likely school

90%

TARGET, LIKELY, OR REALISTIC SCHOOLS

Target, likely, or realistic choices are schools in which you have a moderately high (75 percent) chance of being accepted. These are schools you are the most likely to attend and the application process may involve more work than a highly likely school. You may have to write more essays and the standards for admission are higher, but they are within your range for all of the admissions factors discussed in Chapter 2. These schools are the most realistic ones for you, where you can definitely see yourself committing to and enjoying four years of college.

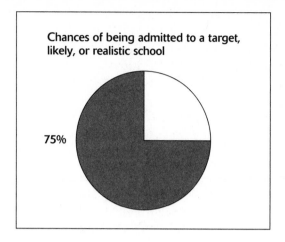

Chances of being admitted to a target, likely, or realistic school

75%

REACH, DREAM, OR UNLIKELY SCHOOLS

Reach, dream, or unlikely schools are colleges that may not be totally within your grasp, because they are so highly selective. Mostly all of the applicants are qualified and these colleges look at many subjective factors (essays, extracurricular activities, letters of recommendations, and others) in addition to objective factors (grades, SAT/ACT scores, and academic program). Because of the highly competitive nature and outstanding reputations of these schools, your chances (25 percent likely) for admission are not guaranteed. These are schools you are not applying to haphazardly, but they are schools you have carefully researched. They have the academic programs and campus life you are seeking. For some students, a *reach* school is an Ivy League institution, a highly selective private university, or a Public Ivy; for other students it is a private or public university which you have heard about and want to attend.

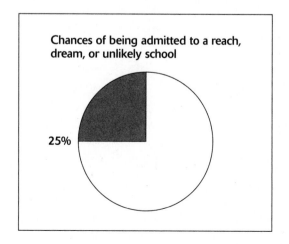

Chances of being admitted to a reach, dream, or unlikely school

25%

How many and what types of schools you apply to depends on your academic history, your financial situation, and your family's wishes. Many students and their families are unrealistic when composing a list of potential colleges. Some families have a "lotto mentality" when it comes to applying to colleges. They believe that their children might gain acceptance by pure luck and that colleges may overlook some of the critical factors in the admissions process. These strategies are extremely unrealistic, and applying to unreasonable choices may be a waste of time and money. In addition, you may be very disappointed if you receive a rejection letter from your dream school, so do not apply randomly to these colleges. Your chances for acceptance will be higher if you can demonstrate a good match between you and the college. Examining the profiles of the entering freshman class on a college's Web site is a good way to see if the college is a reasonable choice for you. Your guidance counselor should be an important resource with whom you can discuss your realistic chances of being admitted. Guidance counselors usually have a good relationship with admissions counselors, so please listen to your counselor. If they don't think you fit the academic profile of a college, it probably isn't a good idea for you to apply.

What are the different admissions plans?

Colleges offer different types of admission plans with varying deadlines and commitment levels. Before discussing each plan, the concept of *yield* needs to be introduced in order for you to understand why some of these plans were developed. *Yield* is the percentage of students who are admitted to an institution who plan to enroll. Colleges need to be able to accurately predict how many students will attend their university, so they have an idea of how many students to accept on early action or early decision plans. Determining a university's yield is actually quite tricky as circumstances (economic and otherwise) change, and universities implement various strategies in order to increase or adjust their yield rate.

If the number of students who plan to attend is higher than anticipated, too many students enroll, which could impact housing, class size, and other campus issues. If too few students agree to enroll, colleges have fewer students than anticipated, and that can also impact the college's budget and other issues. Colleges that under-predict enrollment go to their waitlist (discussed in Chapter 10) to fill up a class to capacity or they may extend admissions deadlines. Students unknowingly can benefit from the unpredictable business of determining an accurate yield rate.

ROLLING ADMISSIONS

Many colleges offer *rolling admissions* plans. There is no specific deadline to apply and students are encouraged to apply to these schools in late summer or early fall. Colleges review these applications as they come in, and you usually receive a decision within four to six weeks. It is suggested that you apply early to these schools, as the freshman class can start filling up rather quickly. There is no downside to applying to schools with rolling admission, as you hear back from these colleges much earlier than other colleges and there is no commitment to attend. Students feel encouraged when they receive an early positive response from a college, and they know that they have one college acceptance under their belt. You definitely need to complete these applications early, so don't delay if you are interested in any of the schools in this category. The admissions standards may be more stringent the later you apply to these schools.

Some Rolling-Admissions Schools

University of Alabama

Arizona State University

City University of New York (CUNY)

Farleigh Dickinson University

Indiana University–Bloomington

Indiana University of Pennsylvania

Johnson & Wales University

Kansas State University

Kettering University

New York Institute of Technology

Pennsylvania State University–University Park

Seton Hall University

University of Colorado–Denver

University of Michigan–Ann Arbor

University of Pittsburgh

University of Rhode Island

EARLY ACTION PLANS

Early action, sometimes called a *priority* application, is a plan where you usually submit your application by November 1, November 15, or December 1. It is a nonbinding application, where you will receive an application decision in January or February, but you will not need to decide if you will attend until May 1. Some colleges also offer a second opportunity to apply early action, referred to as *early action II,* with later deadlines. Early action is my favorite plan, and one of the most popular ways to apply. You obtain early feedback about your application status and it gives you plenty of time to revisit these campuses. Early action applications are increasingly popular, because it gives students the security of an early acceptance without any commitment. There are many colleges which offer this plan, and if you can get your application completed at the beginning of the school year, it is strongly suggested that you apply to schools with early action. If you are not a viable candidate (i.e. below admission standards), you may be rejected or deferred to the regular decision pool and then you will be notified of a final decision in March or April.

The following schools are some of the colleges that offer early action.

Some Early Action Colleges

Adelphi University

Case Western University

Goucher College

Gustavus Adolphus College

Hofstra University

Northeastern University

Rutgers University

State University of New York (SUNY)– Oneonta, New Paltz, Stony Brook

Suffolk University

Tulane University

University of Chicago

University of Connecticut

University of Dallas

University of Maryland–College Park

University of Massachusetts–Amherst

University of North Carolina–Chapel Hill

University of Notre Dame

RESTRICTIVE EARLY ACTION

Restrictive early action, sometimes called *single choice early action,* is similar to early action except that there are some restrictions placed on where else students may apply. Depending on the wording of each college's plan, students in some cases may not be able to apply to other early action schools and/or early decision schools. You typically receive an admissions decision in December or January. These plans differ in the restrictions placed upon you, but they all have one thing in common—you do not have to commit to attend. You still have until May 1 to decide to enroll. If you are accepted under this plan, you can accept their offer at that point or you can see where else you are accepted and then make a decision. As the policies and the schools participating in these programs can change yearly, check with each college directly for specific requirements. As of this writing, Boston College, Georgetown University, Stanford University, and Yale University participate in a restrictive early action plan.

EARLY DECISION

Early decision is a plan where you have decided to apply to one college which you believe is the right school, and, if accepted, you will attend. It is a binding, written agreement where you, a parent, and your guidance counselor usually have to sign to indicate that you understand and abide by the terms of the agreement. Early decision deadlines are usually between November 1 and December 1. Some schools offer *Early Decision II,* a second-chance plan for students who want to commit to an institution, but at a later deadline—usually in January. You can usually apply to other schools, especially those with a rolling or early action deadline. However, if you are accepted to your early decision school, you must immediately withdraw in writing from the other schools to which you applied, whether or not you have received a decision. You receive a financial aid package from your early decision school around the time you get your decision. You can only be released from your early decision agreement if your need for financial aid has not been met by the college and you would not be able to attend with the aid package you received.

If you decide to apply early decision, there are three potential outcomes. The first, happiest, and clearest outcome is that you are admitted to your dream or first-choice school. At that point, you must immediately withdraw from the other colleges to which you applied. A deposit will be required within a short period of time. The other two outcomes are that you may be rejected outright or you may be deferred to the regular decision pool of applicants, where your application will be reviewed again. In both cases, you are released from your agreement, and you are free to apply to other colleges, either for regular decision or to another school for its early decision II deadline (your second-chance early decision school). The following schools are a sample of the colleges that offer early decision plans, although you should check with each institution as policies can change from year to year.

Some Early Decision Schools

American University	Connecticut College
Boston University	Drew University
Clark University	Flagler College

Franklin & Marshall College

Middlebury College

New York University

Pitzer College

Pomona College

Oberlin College

SUNY Buffalo

SUNY Geneseo

Vassar College

Washington University

Washington University in St. Louis

Wesleyan University

Williams College

Virginia Tech

Some Early Decision II Schools

Bowdoin College

Brandeis University

Bryn Mawr College

Carnegie Mellon University

Claremont McKenna College

College of Wooster

Davidson College

Emory University

Grinnell College

Kenyon College

Lehigh University

Macalester College

Reed College

Rensselaer Polytechnic Institute (RPI)

Sarah Lawrence College

Skidmore College

Tufts University

University of Rochester

Vanderbilt University

Washington & Lee University

REGULAR DECISION

Regular decision is a plan where students apply by a set deadline specified by each school. Many colleges have regular decision deadlines by January 15th. You typically receive your decision in March or April and then you have until May 1st to inform colleges of your final selection and to send in a deposit. There are also many colleges which have spring and summer deadlines for students who have not yet applied or who were not accepted to any other schools. A partial list of these schools can be found in Chapter 9.

Should I apply early?

A very common question asked by students and their families is, "Should I apply early?" The answer to this question is not an easy or obvious one, unless you are talking about applying early action. Applying early action is a "no brainer," as long as your application is ready on time.

Applying early decision is a different ballgame. Since early decision is a binding commitment, you should think very carefully before applying early decision. You should also be aware that there are distinct advantages to doing so. It is a wonderful option for students who have researched at least several schools, and who have determined that their first choice school is the right school for them. You can save a lot of time and the cost of application fees by applying early. However, do not rush to apply and do not feel pressured to apply to an early decision school, unless you are absolutely sure that you belong at that school. Applying early can give you a feeling of security, knowing that if you are accepted you have a place to go in the fall. Then you can begin the exciting preparation of getting ready for college, as long as you don't forget about the rest of your senior year.

The decision to apply early should not be made lightly, but only after consulting your family and your guidance counselor. Applying early decision is not the time to forge your parent's signature on this binding contract. Your parents must agree to the financial commitment, although there is a loophole should your financial needs not be met.

Some professionals believe that the early decision option is unfair to students who have not been adequately informed of this option or to those who are not financially comfortable to be able to commit to attending their first choice school. As a result of these concerns, several highly selective colleges, including Harvard, Princeton, and the University of Virginia, have dropped their early decision programs.

One of the main advantages of applying early is that it is commonly known that it is usually easier to be admitted on early decision. Colleges that participate in this program also benefit, because they sometimes take as many as 40 percent of their applicants on early decision. It is a good way for them to build a desirable freshman class, and it gives them the financial security in the early stages of the admissions process.

The chart below highlights the sharp contrast in the percentage of students who were accepted during early decision versus regular decision. These statistics were obtained from each college's Web site, usually in a section entitled "Freshman or Class Profile of 2012" or by searching "Common Data Set," a very useful way to find critical information.

College	% Accepted Early	% Accepted Regular Decision or % of Total Acceptances
Barnard College	48	29
Bowdoin College	30	19
Columbia University	22	7
Cornell University	37	19
Kenyon College	55	29
New York University	33	25
Rice University	30	18
Skidmore College	39	29
Wesleyan University	40	27
Williams College	37	17
University of Pennsylvania	29	17

Road Trip:
Planning Worthwhile Campus Visits

*Construction is booming at a small private university, adding a new gym,
a performing arts center, and a parking garage.*

*A large state university is replacing 40-year-old dorms with beautiful,
new ones.*

*A tour guide at a large private university walks backward the whole tour to
maintain eye contact with prospective students and parents.*

*En route to an information session, parking is so hard to find, a family misses
the information session.*

*A tour guide at a large public university describes the historical significance
of a building's architecture.*

*The dorms in one medium-sized private university are small and
irregularly sized.*

These positive and negative observations can shape your impressions of a college during your visit. Visiting colleges is a fun and educational experience, and it is a critical component of the college admissions process. It can be a bonding experience with your family and a way to learn more about yourself and what you are looking for in a college.

If you have a long list of colleges you are considering, a college visit can help to narrow down the list. Once you set foot on campus, you'll have a much better idea if it's the right school for you and if you can visualize yourself on its campus for four years.

What kind of vibe do you get when you visit?

Although there are many objective factors to consider when making an initial visit, there are intangible factors, such as the vibe you get when you walk around the campus. The adage, "you'll know it when you see it," really describes why guidance counselors strongly suggest that students visit before they apply to colleges. After visiting, you may decide to take a college off your list, or a college may shoot up to the top of your list.

Many students, encouraged by their families, prefer to attend a college within 250 miles of their home. Some students expand their horizons to consider schools within 500 miles from home, and then there are some brave souls who consider colleges over 500 miles from home or on the opposite coast from where they live.

If a family has the time and financial resources to do so, it is wise to visit colleges that you are seriously considering which are far away from home. If you are within 250 miles of a college that interests you, colleges expect that you will visit. Admissions officers want students to be able to state why they want to attend their university. Many college applications have short essays that ask, "What factors have influenced your decision to apply to our university?" (question from a large state university's application) and "Describe the courses of study and the unique characteristics of the University that most interest you? Why do these interests make you a good match for our college?" (question from an Ivy League institution's application). In order to fully answer these questions, you must write about your impressions and interactions during your visit.

When should I visit?

If you are starting the college process early (ninth or tenth grade), you can spread out your visits for when it is convenient for you. It is never too early to start visiting campuses, although many students visit schools in eleventh and twelfth grades.

One of the best times to visit a campus is when classes are in full swing; you'll be able to see the college at its busiest. Optimal times are the fall and spring of your junior year, and the fall and spring of your senior year. If at all possible, visit before you apply. Check each college's calendar as calendars vary widely from school to school. Make sure you are not visiting during any breaks when schools are closed. Do not visit during midterms and finals when students will be too busy to talk to you. If you visit during the week, many high schools excuse your absence, but check with your high school to make sure. Many students and their families like to visit on weekends, because it is convenient for them. Check with the admissions office to make sure they are open. Except for a few classes that meet on weekends, you will not be able to sit in on a class. You will still have the opportunity to talk with students unless most of them go home on weekends.

> Virtual campus tours, videos, and webcams can serve a purpose, but there is no substitute for a campus visit. The only way to determine if a campus has the right vibe is to set foot on the campus and see it firsthand.

The summer between your junior and senior years is a very popular time to visit, although there are some obvious drawbacks to visiting then. Although many colleges do offer summer classes, you will not see the college during its peak time, so don't let that impact your opinion of a college. Many families also combine college visits with a summer vacation, which is fun for the whole family.

If you cannot visit schools before you apply, then you can visit while you're a senior. After you are accepted to college is another good time to plan a visit for the first or second time to assist you in making a final decision of which school to attend. No matter when you visit, you can visit colleges within a logical geographic area. Students on the East Coast, for example, plan trips to colleges in the Boston area, the Washington, D.C. area, the Connecticut area, the New York area, etc. . . .

Just as looking for apartments or houses can be confusing, looking at colleges is also confusing. The best advice is not to visit more than two colleges in a day, as they all become jumbled together in your mind. Taking detailed notes can also alleviate this problem.

How do I arrange a visit?

It is generally not a good idea to visit colleges unannounced. One way that colleges measure your "demonstrated interest" is whether or not you attend an information session and a campus tour, or if you participate in an ambassador program (staying overnight on campus). An information session is usually conducted by an admissions counselor and you are provided with an overview of the academic programs offered, campus life, and the admissions process. Campus tours are usually given by current students, many of whom walk backward during the entire tour. Watching them walk backward is always a highlight of the tour! If a college offers an ambassador-type program, spending a weekend on campus is often the best way to determine if you can see yourself living there.

One of the easiest ways to make arrangements to visit a college is to reserve a tour online. You usually get a confirmation by e-mail, so you know that the reservation went through. You can call the admissions office, if you prefer. Informal arrangements to stay overnight can be made if you know a previous graduate of your high school who is currently attending a college or a sibling of a friend or acquaintance. You can also contact these students to meet you for lunch or to attend classes with them.

What are some tips/strategies for visiting colleges?

In order to have a worthwhile and productive tour, here are some tips and strategies for you to follow during your trip:

- Make sure you sign up for a formal tour, so admissions officers can count your visit as "demonstrated interest."
- Engage your tour guide in relevant conversation about campus life, academics, and safety issues. During your informal conversation, you may learn something you didn't hear during the information session.

- Ask questions of students you see in the cafeteria, milling around the dorms, and walking around the campus.

- Don't be embarrassed by your parents asking questions during the official tour. It's perfectly normal parental behavior.

- Take notes on each college visit. After awhile, you tend to mix up campuses. House hunters videotape houses or apartments to remember the rooms and layouts; apply this concept to campus visits.

> ## Beware of Disorganization
>
> A disorganized campus information session or tour may be a sign that there is a lot of red tape or bureaucracy to wade through, perhaps impacting registration or financial aid. I know of one family who was so turned off by the disorganization of an information session and tour at a large public university that the student decided not to apply to the school.

- Track down students from your high school who are current students and arrange to meet them to get the inside scoop on the campus. Plan this meeting in advance.

- Drop by to say an informal hello to your high school's college representative (if you have one) if you can't arrange an interview during your campus visit or if the college doesn't permit interviews. Before you visit, ask your guidance counselor for the name of your college representative.

- Don't ask basic questions such as, "How many students do you have?" during an information session. You should already know the answers to basic questions from doing initial research on a college's Web site before your campus visit.

- Get the names and e-mail addresses of the tour guide and leader of the information session so you can thank them and ask them further questions.

- Get copies of school and local newspapers to get a sense of the issues and the tone of the campus.

- Visit the campus bookstore, where textbooks, college apparel, and other paraphernalia are sold. Many students like to buy souvenirs, such as T-shirts, sweatshirts, banners, teddy bears, or mugs.

- Visit the nearby town or city to see what cultural activities and shopping areas are nearby.

- Pick up course catalogs and other materials available in the admissions office.

For Parents Regarding the Campus Visit Tour

Some specific information that parents should be aware of during the tour:

❏ Make sure you sign up for a formal tour, so admissions officers can count your visit as "demonstrated interest."

❏ Let your son or daughter ask most of the questions during a college visit; this may be hard, but try to control yourself.

❏ Ask an admissions officer about obtaining a free food voucher so you can try the food.

❏ Keep in mind that the dorm rooms shown during a tour may not be freshman dorms or they may be the nicer or newer dorms, not one your child may have for freshman year.

❏ Ask yourself if you can picture your child living on this campus, walking around like the other students. You know your son or daughter better than anyone.

❏ Determine how your child will get home from this college. Will he or she have difficulty finding transportation for holidays or visits, or is transportation easily accessible? One state university system provides buses home to convenient centralized locations at a reasonable cost.

❏ Look around for blue light systems and the presence of security guards or local police to determine how committed this college is to campus safety and the security of its students. How many incidents were reported in the last year?

What questions should I ask?

Many of your questions will be answered by an information session and campus tour. However, you want to get beyond some of the superficial information and dig deeper in order to really compare colleges that you visit. Through direct observation or by asking questions, you want to determine the answers to the following questions about academic life, campus life, and the campus facilities and the extended community. Parents can ask some questions too, but it really is time for you to start advocating for yourself, so now is not the time to be shy about asking what you really want to know.

EVALUATING THE ACADEMIC LIFE

One of your primary concerns when visiting is to evaluate the academic programs, policies, and reputation of a college, as well as the quality of its professors. The following questions can be asked of students, faculty members, and admissions officers to determine if the academic life best suits your needs:

- What is the average amount of time students devote outside of class to studying?
- Are you being intellectually challenged? (ask current students if they are)
- How accessible are professors? Do they post office hours and give out their e-mail addresses?
- Are teaching assistants used in addition to professors?
- What majors or programs of study are available? How easy is it to change a major?
- Are advisors knowledgeable and easily available for appointments?
- What is registration like? Can you register online or do you have to wait in a long line?
- How often do freshmen get closed out of classes? What is the procedure for getting into a class you must take for your major?
- Is undergraduate research encouraged? Are research and internship opportunities well advertised?
- Can you transfer between colleges within a university if you have been admitted to a particular area of study?
- Which departments are the strongest, weakest, and most highly funded?
- What is the grading policy of the university?
- What are the acceptance rates to law school, medical school, and other graduate programs?
- Is there a minimum GPA that must be maintained in order to live on campus or to stay in an academic or athletic program?
- Is there a freshman retention program in place to assist freshman during the first few months of transition to college life?

EVALUATING THE CAMPUS LIFE

Campus life is as important as the academic life of a college. If you are going to live on campus, you need to obtain information about housing, meal plans, and social and cultural activities. If you are going to commute, you need to know where to park, and how you can ensure you are connected to activities on campus. When you visit, get a feel for the political and social climates of the school.

- Are the dorms spacious or cramped? How are dorms allocated? Is there a lottery system in place? Is housing guaranteed all four years?
- What types of food plans are available? Is the food good, passable, or lousy?
- Is this a commuter school? Does the college empty out on weekends? What is parking like? On many campuses, parking can be a nightmare.

- Do the students look happy or bored?
- Are there any events occurring on campus or do you have to leave campus to have a social life?
- Is there a Greek life? What percent of the student body participates in sororities and fraternities?
- What clubs and organizations does the college have? Are there religious services for you?
- What is the political climate of the campus?
- Does every student look identical or is it a diverse campus?
- Are there parties every night on campus? Do parties begin on Thursday nights?
- What is the alcohol policy and is the policy enforced?

EVALUATING THE CAMPUS FACILITIES AND THE EXTENDED COMMUNITY

In addition to academic and campus life, consider the physical attributes of the campus, as well as the atmosphere of the surrounding community. You should check whether the physical campus is in a state of neglect or whether there are attempts to attract students with renovation projects or new construction. A college's relationship with the surrounding community can enhance students' experiences during their four years.

> What does this college boast about? Is it the library, sports teams, unusual majors, community involvement, internships, co-op programs, or undergraduate research? Is the college adding undergraduate or graduate programs?

- Is the physical campus in good shape? Do the heating and cooling systems work properly? Are there fire alarms and sprinkler systems in the dorms?
- Are the library hours convenient for all students? Colleges love to brag about how many books they have in their collection. Do they have an inter-library loan policy for materials not easily available?
- If the campus is experiencing growth, is construction visible? What is being built and what is the expected timeframe for completion? How disruptive will construction be?
- What types of relationships do the college students have with the local community? Are students welcomed into local stores and businesses?
- Are there cultural events nearby, and are they at a reduced or reasonable fee for students?
- Is transportation available to the nearest town or city? One large state university offers free transportation throughout the city.
- Are shuttles on the college campus frequent enough so students are not late for classes?

After you get back from your trip, don't forget to send a thank you note to any admissions officers you met. The Boston College Web site offers excellent advice to students visiting colleges. It suggests that you stick around after the official tour ends to make informal visits to the library, dining hall, and other places of interest.

A college visit can reinforce your choice of a college. After visiting and determining the answers to the above questions, you gain valuable information about where on your list a college is rated. As you visit each college, you should be asking yourself, "Would I be happy at what I think is my probable or highly likely school? Did I dislike my reach school, and now after visiting should I take it off my list and apply elsewhere?"

Chart for note taking

There is so much to see and do during a campus visit that it can get very confusing and you may tend to mix up the colleges you have seen. During or after the tour, it is very helpful to take notes so you can review them later. The following chart can help you keep track of the schools you are visiting. If you're a logical, list-happy person who makes decisions based on facts, you can get very elaborate and rate each college on a scale from one star (lowest rating) to five stars (highest rating). If you're someone who makes decisions based on feelings, you can just jot down how you felt about something or simply check each item. Either method is perfectly acceptable.

Use a five-star rating or jot down your notes for each college.

Criteria	College 1	College 2	College 3	College 4	College 5
Size					
Location					
Public vs. Private					

Criteria	College 1	College 2	College 3	College 4	College 5
Academic Programs					
Student Diversity					
Male/Female Ratio					
Athletics					
Cost					
Admissions Standards/ Selectivity					
Facilities/ Technology					

continued

Criteria	College 1	College 2	College 3	College 4	College 5
Family Issues					
Disability Services					
Study Abroad/ Co-ops/ Internships					
Nearby Town/ City/ Shopping/ Cultural Activities					
Can you visualize yourself here?					
What are your family's impressions?					

Criteria	College 1	College 2	College 3	College 4	College 5
What are your favorite things about this campus?					
What are your least favorite things about this campus?					
What are your overall impressions?					

How to Write a Winning Personal Statement

"An essay should be well written, concise, and insightful. A student does not have to have swum the English Channel or climbed Mt. Everest to make a good impression in an essay. Some of the simplest student accomplishments, when explained directly and well, have been the most impressive."

–Nancy J. Maly, Director of Admissions, Grinnell College

As I discussed in Chapter 2, the personal statement or essay provides you with an opportunity to convey your passions, interests, and values to the admissions officer reading your application. The words *personal statement* and *essay* are used interchangeably to refer to the long main essay required for many applications. Shorter essays may also be required on some applications. The essay is particularly important for admission to highly selective colleges.

The goal of the personal statement or essay is to demonstrate that you are a decent writer who is ready for college-level work, and to express something about you that is not obvious from the rest of your application. You also want to directly or indirectly state why you want to attend a particular college, although this information may be contained in a short essay.

As the quote above indicates, the personal statement is an opportunity to share information and insights about yourself that are not evident from the rest of your application. The personal statement or essay does not have to be perfect; it just has to honestly reflect who you are and what you're thinking.

Essays are an important factor in the admissions process, and it is one area that is totally within your control. Spending a lot of time on your personal statement can have a big payoff. If you are an average student, a well-thought-out essay can push you over the edge if you're borderline in terms of your admissions standards. I know a student who had borderline grades and SAT scores, but the admissions director was so impressed with her essay that she accepted the student because of her passionate writing. Essays also carry a lot of weight with highly selective colleges, so take your time and write one that is insightful and interesting.

Almost every student has heard her English teacher say, "Show, don't tell!" when writing any type of essay. Your teacher would be right! Don't *tell* someone you have great leadership skills. Instead, show them by recounting your experience as a Big Brother/Big Sister and explaining how the experience inspired you and impacted you in some way. As one of the admissions directors said, you don't have to climb Mt. Everest or talk about a traumatic, life-altering event for your essay to be successful. Who doesn't like *Seinfeld,* the television show about nothing? The show is really about the daily, trivial aspects of life, which are sometimes the most interesting and captivating. The same can be true about your personal statement. It's not what you write, but how you write it. Does the essay convey your ideals, impressions, and experiences? If it does, then your essay is an effective one. Would someone who knows you well and reads your essay say, "Yes, this essay captures the essence of John Smith."

> Many students stress about the essay; they find it very difficult to identify an essay topic and to actually write the essay itself. Some students go so far as to buy essays online or have others write the essay for them, including hiring professional essay writers who can charge several hundred dollars. Do not do this! Professionally written essays are very easy to spot. If your guidance counselor can spot them (and she will), you can be sure that college admissions counselors will also spot them.

A personal statement is usually about 500 words and approximately one page. Many students worry if their essay is 10 words under or 50 words over the limit. College admissions counselors are not sitting there counting your words. If it's about a page, slightly under or slightly over, they will read it as long as it's interesting. The ideal time to write a personal statement is the summer between your junior and senior years.

What are some common essay questions?

Many colleges keep the same essay questions for many years, while others change the questions every year or every few years. College applications are usually available beginning in August, so find out the essay topic of each school you are applying to, unless the college participates in the Common Application© or the Universal College Application.

COMMON APPLICATION TOPICS

The topics on the Common Application are the essays you use if you apply using this service, which is free to students. There are currently six essay topics from which you can choose. You are instructed to write a minimum of 250 words on the following prompts:

Common Application Essay Topics	
1.	Evaluate a significant experience, achievement, risk you have taken, or ethical dilemma you have faced and its impact on you.
2.	Discuss some issue of personal, local, national, or international concern and its importance to you.
3.	Indicate a person who has had a significant influence on you, and describe that influence.
4.	Describe a character in fiction, a historical figure, or a creative work (as in art, music, science, etc.) that has had an influence on you, and explain that influence.
5.	A range of academic interests, personal perspectives, and life experiences adds much to the educational mix. Given your personal background, describe an experience that illustrates what you would bring to the diversity in a college community, or an encounter that demonstrated the importance of diversity to you.
6.	Topic of your choice.

The personal statement from the Universal College Application by ApplicationsOnline, LLC, is limited to 500 words and the prompt is:

> Please write an essay (500 words or fewer) that demonstrates your ability to develop and communicate your thoughts. Some ideas include: a person you admire; a life-changing experience; or your viewpoint on a particular current event.

As you can see, the questions on these applications are quite similar and they are broad enough that you can really write about almost anything!

If you choose to use the Common Application or Universal College Application, many colleges require you to write additional essays on a college's supplement, which is an addendum to these applications. If you choose not to use the Common Application or Universal College Application, you can apply using the college's own application, if it has one.

The essay prompts you will be given are general enough so you have plenty of leeway to write about what you want, especially if you choose the "topic of your choice" essay. It is strongly suggested that you don't pick something too controversial, such as politics, abortion, or gay rights, because you don't know who's reading your essay and where they're coming from. The best advice is to write about what you know and what you're passionate about. Sometimes the most trivial, everyday topic in your life is the easiest to write about, especially if you put your own spin on it.

COLLEGE APPLICATION ESSAY TOPICS

Some possible essay topics are as follows:

- Personal illness (Diabetes, ADHD, colitis—don't give details about the illness, but its impact on you academically, socially, etc.)

- Distinctive personal characteristics (Being short or tall, having freckles, having red hair—these traits tend to be humorous; focus on the impact it has on you.)

- Research (What did you learn when you participated in a summer research program?)

- Internship (Share what you learned from an internship.)

- Summer experiences (Tell of the impact of your interesting summer experience. Be careful here. Admissions counselors get tired of Habitat for Humanity essays or camp stories, unless you can talk specifically about the effect the experience had on you or how it has changed your thoughts and beliefs.)

- Books (Do not summarize the story, but describe how you are similar or dissimilar to a character, or how the book affected or changed your opinion.)

- Art, music, creative writing (Explain how it makes you feel or how it's an important part of your life.)

- Hobbies (Karate, yoga, fencing—express how it makes you feel or how it builds your confidence.)

- Sports (Stay away from sports essays, unless it's a very unusual aspect about sports. One student wrote about how much he learned from sitting on the bench all season.)

- Areas of passion (Write about anything you're passionate about and why.)

- The "Seinfeld" essay (Choose everyday events, such as shoes, chocolate milk, Wite Out, snowflakes, cooking, being a twin, or being the only boy in the family. Sometimes these are the most clever and interesting essays, if they are well written.)

- Work experiences (What did you learn as a supermarket checker, an employee at Starbucks Coffee, or a shoe salesperson?)

Admissions counselors read hundreds if not thousands of essays a year. While it is not your job to entertain or to put a smile on their faces, you do want to write an essay that holds their interest. The first line, in particular, should be intriguing and attention grabbing. Some actual student essays are evaluated later in this chapter.

While it can be a family effort to come up with a topic, read, and edit your essay, admissions counselors truly want to read an essay written by a 17 year old. In other words, write it yourself and don't use a thesaurus. Big words don't impress anyone, and it's not usually believable that a 17 year old would use SAT words on a regular basis. If you got an 800 on your SAT/ACT reading section, your essay *might* be a little more sophisticated than someone who got a 500 on their SAT/ACT reading section. If you normally use big words, go ahead and use them if that's normal behavior for you. As long as your work is consistent with other written material you've used in the application, admissions officers won't necessarily think you borrowed the language from other sources. Just consider that if your essay is too good for your testing score, colleges may suspect you didn't write it. Also, keep in mind that colleges now have the ability to compare your personal statement with your essay from your SAT or ACT exam, especially if they have any doubt as to the authorship of your personal statement.

What Are Admissions Counselors Looking For?

Admissions counselors give the following advice about what they are looking for in a personal statement and what makes an effective essay.

"The application essay is a great way to grab the attention of the admissions committee and to help us get to know you on a more personal level. We look for ideas that are well thought out, sincerely written, and filled with expressive and descriptive words that create a vivid story. Also, if you've dealt with a particular challenge that may have affected your academic performance, the personal statement is your chance to share that information with us. Admissions counselors have your application in front of them, you don't have to list every activity you've been involved in or talk about your grades. Here's your chance to tell them something they can't get from your transcript. Get personal! And, of course, triple check for spelling mistakes and make sure to use good grammar. And make sure you answer the essay question—don't stray or make your focus too wide."–Cheryl Brown, Director of Undergraduate Admissions, Binghamton University, State University of New York

"The personal statement should give us a good picture as to why the student wants to attend Rensselaer but also tells us a little about them that we cannot discern from the application. For example, the personal statement is a good place to talk about core values or their passion for a particular field. The essay can also be a good place to talk about character, particularly if it related to an organization they have been involved with or found particularly important in their lives. Students who mention that they worked hard to achieve the Gold Award of the Girl Scouts of America may be surprised to learn once they have been admitted that they have earned a scholarship specifically for Gold Award winners. The essay can be a good place to list those 'intangibles' which merit recognition by an admissions committee or a financial aid committee." –Raymond Lutzky, Director, Outreach and Associate Director, Enrollment, Rensselaer Polytechnic Institute (RPI)

"Truly, I want to know the soul of the applicant. In other words, is the applicant writing from the heart? Is the applicant answering the question(s) being asked? Has the applicant given some serious thought to the question being asked? Has the applicant given any thought to the reader? Remember, some of the best essays noted by admissions counselors at national and regional conferences tend to come from students who write from experience, and from the heart, and who write well; you need to hear the writer's voice." –Mitchell Thompson, Dean of Students, Scarsdale High School, Former Associate Dean of Admissions and Records for The Cooper Union, Former Assistant Director for Admissions at Oneonta College, SUNY

How do I get started?

Now that you have a sense of possible topic areas, how do you get started? You can ask parents, family members, and friends for their opinions on potential essay topics. It can be very useful to have a brainstorming session with your family. You need about 15–20 minutes in a quiet place where everyone is focused on you and your essay. Have someone serve as the secretary and jot down ideas, while you and your family come up with as many ideas as you can within the time period. Do not screen the ideas; your job is to just generate as many possible topics as possible. After the brainstorming session, you can review the list with or without your family and narrow down the list to three to five potential topics. Then discuss the merits of each idea, keeping in mind the goals of an effective essay, mentioned earlier in this chapter. Keep working through the ideas until you come up with what you think is the best topic for your personal statement. Save the runners up for other essays you may need to write.

Now comes the hard part, the actual writing of the essay. The hardest part is the first sentence, after that it gets slightly easier. I have seen many students procrastinate writing their essays. Do not leave it until the last possible moment, as you want to have a chance to edit and revise your essay. You may have to force yourself to sit down and write the first draft. Just as in the brainstorming session, don't screen your first draft. Instead, just write and let your ideas flow. Some students need total silence to write, others need background noise, such as the TV or their IPod. Some students like to write an outline first, others prefer to wing it. Whichever style suits you, just try to complete a first draft in one sitting, if possible. Then let your essay incubate. Leave the essay alone for a day or two. Don't worry, you'll still be thinking about it. Take another look at it from a fresh perspective, and at that point you can start editing and revising the essay several times. Do a final proofread and then you're ready for your harshest critics: your family, your English teacher, and your guidance counselor. You can incorporate all of their suggestions, but only if they make sense to you. Make sure you are answering the question from the essay prompt. Also, remember not to purposely use big words and to use the voice of a 17 year old. It's your essay, so, as it says in *Hamlet*, "to thine own self be true."

> **TIP:** When writing an essay, have a brainstorming session to come up with ideas. Generate as many ideas as possible. Narrow down the list until you come up with your #1 essay topic. Write your first draft in one sitting and then let your ideas incubate for a day or two; next, take a fresh look at your essay and revise, edit, and proofread. When you're ready, show your essay to a few select people.

How do I make my essay stand out?

The pressure is on to write a terrific (but not perfect) essay. But how do you distinguish yourself from everyone else applying? Since many applicants have similar grades and SAT/ACT scores, the essay is a golden opportunity to "stand out." You can stand out by developing a well-written essay on any topic. If you write about something that highlights your personality or something about which you're genuinely passionate, your essay complements the rest of your application. If your essay is sincere, persuasive, and written from the heart, you should be in pretty good shape. If you've gotten across your impressions, values, and what's really important to you, then you probably have done what you needed to do. Do not focus on trying to impress people, as it will not come across as sincere. As our admissions directors have suggested, be personal and allow admissions counselors to see your soul. As Raymond Lutzky from Rensselaer Polytechnic Institute (RPI) says, "ultimately painting a positive picture of your best qualities should be the direction for an essay. Ideally, a student should show their best characteristics rather than attempting to make a great philosophical point."

If you're a funny person, a humorous essay may come naturally to you. If you're not known as a funny person, don't even attempt a humorous essay. Just remember, the essay is about you. Even if you write an essay about how your grandmother inspires you, don't say too much about your grandmother's story or history. Instead, get across what you've inherited from her, what you've learned from her experiences, and how she has impacted your life. It sounds selfish, but the emphasis should always be on you.

Use descriptive words and give vivid details. Remember, you want to catch the reader's attention with great opening sentences, so editing is really important. Try to stick to one page, as admissions counselors have many essays to read. Don't be repetitive and try to link your ending to your opening. It's also a good idea to take an objective look at your essay. Take a step back and put yourself in the reader's shoes. Does the essay capture your interest? Is the essay passionate? Do you get a clear sense of the writer's personality and priorities? Have you learned something new that you wouldn't have gleaned from the rest of the application? Don't be obsessed about being unique. Your goal is to give readers an honest portrayal of who you are. If you do all of these things, you will successfully write a winning personal statement.

What are some do's and don'ts about essay writing?

There are some definite do's and don'ts when writing the personal statement and answering other essay questions.

Some do's

- Be sure to answer the essay question; don't stray too far off the topic.
- Show, don't tell.
- Demonstrate, with specific examples, your interest in a college.
- Incubate or think about your first draft for a few days.
- Revise and proofread many times.
- Show your essay to family members, your English teacher, and your guidance counselor.
- Use the voice of a 17 year old.
- Share any challenges or obstacles that may have impacted your academic performance.
- "Be your own advocate. Take risks in your responses to essay questions."—Mitchell Thompson, Scarsdale High School and former admissions counselor
- Be yourself!

Some don'ts

- 🎓 Don't discuss something that is too controversial.
- 🎓 Avoid clichés.
- 🎓 Don't name the wrong college in your essay. If you are applying to the University of Rochester, don't say, ". . . and I really want to attend the University of Scranton because . . ." This mistake can cost you dearly, so be very careful when proofreading your essay.
- 🎓 Don't use gimmicks, sending gifts or other things with your essay.
- 🎓 Don't tell a story or focus on other people too much.
- 🎓 Don't repeat what's in the rest of your application.
- 🎓 Don't hire anyone to write your essay.
- 🎓 Don't use a thesaurus, and avoid big words unless you really use them and you know what they mean.

Some topics to avoid

- 🎓 "Avoid writing angry essays."–(Raymond Lutzky, RPI) If you write about how you are upset about the lack of funding for stem cell research, you may offend some readers with your political leanings. Be passionate in your essay, but be careful not to show anger about issues dear to your heart where others may have a different opinion.
- 🎓 "Avoid essays where the end result is that the reader should feel badly for the applicant. Some students attempt to shock or make the reader feel guilty."–(Raymond Lutzky) If you have suffered from a serious illness, you do not want the reader to feel sorry for you. The essay can emphasize how you have overcome your obstacles.
- 🎓 "Avoid self-aggrandizing or boastful essays."–(Nancy J. Maly, Grinnell) If you are the winner of a prestigious contest or competition, stress your accomplishments in such a way that you do not come across as showing off or acting conceited.
- 🎓 "Avoid maudlin or sad topics, such as death, violence, divorce."–(Nancy J. Maly) Be careful writing about sad events, as counselors read many of these essays. If your essay has a different slant to it, you can attempt the topic; otherwise stay away from very sad or depressing topics.
- 🎓 "Don't make assumptions regarding what admissions officers want to know."–(Mitchell Thompson) Be genuine, and write about what's important to you. Don't pick a topic because you think it's what the reader wants to hear.

How do I respond to short-answer essays?

Many students write one personal statement and then reuse this essay for most of their schools, especially if they are using the Universal College Application or the Common Application. Many colleges still require you to use their school's supplement, which can consist of several short-answer essays. Your responses to these questions can range from a few sentences to one or two long paragraphs.

Here are some common questions that require short answers:

"Tell us more about one of your extracurricular, volunteer, or employment activities (100–150 words) " (Universal College Application by ApplicationsOnline, LLC)

"Tell us about your potential major or area of interest and your reasons for applying to _____."

"What contributions do you see yourself making to our university?"

Your response to these questions should include the academic areas you are considering during college. If you are fairly positive about being a psychology major, go ahead and answer as such. If you know that you are interested in the sciences, but you don't know which particular area yet, just go ahead and write about your love for science, backed up by the things you have done in high school to support that interest. Your response can be a little more general, as long as you get across your general passion for the sciences. If you don't have a clear focus, that's okay, too, but do give a general area of interest. Colleges understand that you may change your major when you get there or a few more times once you are in college. Also, anything you mention in these short essays should also be included on your résumé (more about that in Chapter 6).

How should you answer a question that asks why are you interested in a college? You are being given a golden opportunity to demonstrate your knowledge and interest in the college. This is a very important question as colleges want an indication of your "demonstrated interest." They want to get a sense of whether or not you will attend their school if you are accepted (remember the concept of yield?). The best time to answer this question is after you've done your research and after a campus visit. Admissions counselors don't want to hear that their college campus is in a particular city; they already know that. They want to hear, in specific terms, what you like about their school. You can talk about a professor you met, a class you attended, a particular research lab they have, and other details that substantiate your knowledge and interest. Don't tell colleges what you think they want to hear. Make genuine choices of potential colleges and really consider why you want to attend that particular college. Both you and the college are looking for the right match. You may be qualified for a particular school, but does it really fit your needs?

Other examples of short essays are:

"Describe a challenge you have faced and how you overcame it."

"Describe an experience with a cultural, social, or ethnic group other than your own and its impact on you."

"Why is attending college important to you?"

"Describe one of your areas of strength and how it impacts your life."

"If you were a contestant on a reality TV show, which show would be the best fit for you?"

"What do you do in your spare time? What are some of your hobbies or interests?"

These essays may be even more difficult and riskier for you to answer than the personal statement. You are being asked to identify a potential shortcoming and some very personal information. It could be that the riskier and more personal the question, the more enriching your answer may be. Some students may be offended or scared away by some of these questions, whereas other students may say, "Wow! This is the kind of school I've been looking for."

Simply looking at a college's essay questions can give you some insight as to whether a college is a good fit. How do you answer these questions? The good news is that there really are no right or wrong answers. You answer them by assessing yourself and answering them honestly. Don't try to guess what admissions counselors want you to say, but do make sure your answer is clear and actually answers the question. Answer these questions as you would a personal statement; by taking your time, editing and proofreading them, and showing them to others whose opinions you value.

Other types of short essays can be in the form of "fill in the blank" questions:

1. If I were given three wishes, I would wish for _____, _____, and _____.

2. If I could meet with any historical or fictional person, it would be _____.

3. _____ is important to me.

4. I wish I could _____.

5. The one thing I would like the Admissions Committee to know about me is_____
   _____.

These types of questions bode well for creative individuals; others may dread them. You can have fun with these questions, and they are a great way for admissions counselors to get a snapshot of your personality.

Sample personal statements and critiques

The following four personal statements are actual student essays, which are printed in their entirety. Following each essay is a critique to determine if the essay lived up to the standards of a winning personal statement, as discussed in the previous sections. Keep in mind that the remarks in the critiques are subjective; readers are free to disagree. A checklist for any type of essay can be found at the end of this chapter.

Personal Statement #1

The student who wrote Personal Statement #1 now attends an Ivy League institution. The student is interested in the field of English and creative writing. The expectations for his essay would be high, as you would anticipate his essay to be creative and well written. You can judge for yourself.

There comes a time in every man's life when he must answer a character-defining question: If you could have a super power, what would it be? This hypothetical subject has been debated among underage heroes for centuries; it has been heard on playgrounds, in tree houses, and under manholes all over the planet. Its answers come as varied as transliterated spellings of "Hanukkah."

There are a few timeless responses: flight, invisibility, pyrokinesis, and mind control are oft-mentioned favorites. Man has longed to possess these four since the Stone Age to tackle his most fundamental problems—moving, hunting, keeping warm, and reproducing, respectively. Luckily, these powers still come in handy for our present-day needs, such as rescuing damsels from the tops of tall buildings, sneaking past bouncers at no-goodniks' exclusive clubs, breaking into evildoers' ice-palace lairs, and infiltrating enemy brains to prevent the release of kittens with laser eyes upon our helpless country.

But my ideal super power is something far more unexpected and subtle in its, well, superness, than the usual examples. If I could have a super power, I would choose the ability to turn into a zebra.

Now you may be thinking, "What do zebras have that a lion or a gorilla or a great white shark doesn't?" If this were based on raw power alone, I concede that the zebra would not have been my first choice. But I'm no teeth-and-muscle purist: The reason I'd choose zebras isn't for their incredible stamina, or their vicious bites and fatal kicks, or their binocularlike vision and incredible hearing, or their clever form of camouflage, or the way they zigzag to escape from predators, or even their excellent parenting. I'd choose zebras for a certain element called *style* that is simply lacking in other animals.

When a zebra glides into a room, all creatures present stop what they're doing, be they human, giraffe, or even fellow zebra. The lion may be king of the jungle, but the zebra is its soul. The mere sight of a zebra has led some to preposterous ends: Equids of all types mate with zebras to get that telltale "z" in their child's name, producing endless combinations of zebroids—zorses, zonies, zeebrasses, and even zeedonks are recorded in Darwin's raunchiest annals. Lord Rothschild was known to ride a zebra-drawn carriage through London to boost his reputation as a noble eccentric. It is a well-regarded opinion among music historians that zebras were the driving force behind jazz.

While the last claim may not be true, the zebra has such silent singularity that it stands out in any list of mammals. This quiet uniqueness reminds me of myself in some ways—it's nary a peculiar day to see me in a public space wearing a black sock on one foot and a white on the other, or a pirate hat on my head, or a plush snake in my shirt pocket, or a cape around my neck. I suppose it's my desire to stand out, to zigzag like the zebra instead of bolting straight ahead, that so attracts me to that noble animal.

So the next time there are wrongs to right and you need a fantastic alter ego to change into, don't opt for the same old superfast, superstrong Human 2.0 we'll probably evolve into soon enough anyway: Turn into someone stripier than ordinary. Who said justice wasn't black and white?

Personal Statement #1 Critique

The "zebra" essay was used as a model in English classes and was passed around the school as an example of an outstanding essay. It is very creative and well written. The opening is clever and encourages the reader to continue reading. Posing a question and answering it is a good strategy. The writer uses very descriptive words and great visual imagery, as well as actual details about a zebra. The reader gets a very good idea that the writer is a colorful, independent, and zany individual. It is enjoyable to read, and in addition to writing, it is clear that the student also enjoys animals, science, and history. There is a 17-year-old voice present, although the student is a sophisticated writer. The reader comes away with a sense that the writer is very talented with a potentially very bright future.

Although doing so only briefly, the writer does relate the zebra to himself. Other essays may be more direct about the student's career interests. It is very clear that we have learned something new about the student, and that he is a passionate and creative writer. Without any doubt, he did the job he needed to do!

PERSONAL STATEMENT #2

The student who wrote Personal Statement #2 is attending an honors program in a medium-sized public college. She has self-identified as being a candidate for a dietetics program, which is science oriented. While the student could write about any topic, she chose to focus on why she is interested in pursuing a career in dietetics.

> Science Honor Society was a goal I wished to fulfill during my junior year of high school. I had the grades and hard work, yet I still needed an extra science-related activity to become eligible for admittance. I decided to volunteer at a nearby hospital. At first, I was a little nervous, since I did not know what the experience would be like or the type of work I would be doing. However, after only a couple of weeks on the job, I learned the ropes of the hospital and became comfortable in its environment. As a volunteer, I am a messenger, responsible for picking up patients' prescriptions at the pharmacy, getting blood from the blood bank, or doing any other favor that a nurse or hospital employee needs. On some days, I work in medical records, sorting patients' files accordingly, while on other days, I visit patients, bringing them magazines to read or assisting in the discharge process in helping the patients begin a safe trip home. I not only see how important it is to have people willing to help others, but I see how everyone working in the hospital is a family of people who work day in and day out making the lives of patients more comfortable and secure and knowing that their health is in good hands.
>
> There are some volunteers at the hospital who have been working for nearly twenty years. I see these individuals as being dedicated, which I too have gained from this experience through my 80 hours and 7 months of work thus far. This drive to help others and succeed in a task is something I will bring with me in whatever situations I encounter in the future. When I graduate from college, I intend to be a part of this magic of working in the health profession as a dietician, making meal plans to meet

patients specific needs and teaching patients how to eat right in order to remain healthy, become healthy if not already, and live a life of longevity. I have been interested in nutrition for the past few years. It is important to me that I know which foods are healthy and which are deleterious, so I can in turn eat right, be healthy, and remain this way for the rest of my life. I have and will continue to pass on good habits to my family and eventually to my patients as well.

Working in the hospital allows me to see the type of environment I will be working in when I get older, since the hospital is one sector in which dieticians work. Even though I began volunteering at the hospital to meet a requirement for Science Honor Society, I now see that volunteering is rewarding to experience the joy of a day's work, a place of camaraderie to make new friends with people who want to help others just as I do, and it is a way for me to look at my future and see that I will be helping others. It is not just spending time out of the house after school and during the summer, but an adventure that I will treasure forever.

Personal Statement #2 Critique

Personal Statement #2 is a very focused essay, which provides the reader with the rationale in applying to a very specific program. The message is clear, and it is written in the voice of a 17 year old. It is persuasive, and definitely written from the heart. It conveys the impact working in a hospital had on the student and that the student is passionate about her prospective field. Although her opening sentence could have been more hard-hitting and some of her images more vivid, Personal Statement #2 is a strong essay that definitely answered the question about the writer's interest in the dietetics field.

PERSONAL STATEMENT # 3

The student who wrote Personal Statement #3 is a dual citizen, born and raised until the age of 11 in England. The student is interested in a career as a writer, but he also has a stated interest in drama. He is attending a large public university in a state different from his own.

English children are taught by their mums that "Good children should be seen and not heard." Growing up in England, I was always a proper little gentleman, even though my parents introduced me at a relatively young age to theater, an art form in which people must be both seen *and* heard. Nonetheless, somewhere in my child's mind, I knew that I wanted to be involved in the magic that is theater.

Fast forward. Having moved to America at the age of eleven, I was trying to adapt to a culturally foreign lifestyle: No afternoon tea, no one to play cricket with, but sunshine instead of rain! I remember sitting in classes, always wanting to participate, but holding back, remembering what I had been taught back home. When I was encouraged to read the part of an American rancher in John Steinbeck's *Of Mice and Men*, I saw an entire class mesmerized by my reading, detailing Steinbeck's theme of one's struggle to identify one's place in the universe. They could not imagine how I had changed my voice from a British accent, to that of a Western rancher. From that point on, and throughout high school, I became an integral part of the drama program.

In addition to performing in theater, I also enjoy attending it. A few months ago, I went to a performance of the musical, *Passing Strange*. The experience was life altering. A line in a song by Stew, writer of *Passing Strange*, states, "Life is a mistake that only art can correct." Hearing this touched my soul, and clinched my future for me. I realized that I no longer wanted to be a professional actor, but I yearned to put my own stamp on the artistic world, through things that I create, rather than acting out someone else's words. My direction became clear: I want to be a writer.

My first real writing opportunity came in July 2008, when I returned to _____, a performing arts summer program. _____ recently introduced a contest for student-written, 10-minute plays. I got to work, writing draft after draft of what eventually became *The Death of James* [the name of the play has been changed], a play about how the decisions we make deeply impact our lives. I submitted the play, and it was selected as one of five to be performed by campers, and directed by the authors. Just when I thought that this was life's perfect moment, I learned that _____ Publishing Company was publishing my play in a book of anthologies. I am still over the moon.

While this is an accomplishment I am very proud of, I realize that I still have many years of learning and developing my art ahead of me. I am hoping to hone my writing skills by attending the (college name). I wish to embark upon a journey that I know has many challenges and all types of surprises. If it is true that "Life is a mistake that only art can correct," then I am very anxious to begin making my contribution.

Personal Statement #3 Critique

The jargon from England is endearing, and that is definitely part of the charm of this essay. It is interesting for the reader to hear about different cultural practices. The imagery is vivid and descriptive. It is obvious that the student has a passion for writing and theater. The essay clearly conveys the writer's intention in pursuing his craft. The student tells the reader about his play, which received recognition from a publishing company, but it is not boastful in any way. It is a very passionate and effective essay.

One possible improvement to the essay is that if you are going to mention the school's name in the essay, you can state in detail why that particular university meets your needs. For example, you can mention a particular department, a professor's name, or a production group or school newspaper you intend to join when you get on campus.

PERSONAL STATEMENT #4

Personal Statement #4 is another career-oriented essay, which states why the student is interested in business as a college major. The student is attending an honors program in a small, private university.

When I was thirteen, the thing I wanted most in life was a limited edition, glow-in-the-dark Power Rangers snow globe. The local hobby shop charged an astronomical amount for the snow globe because it was such a rare piece; there were only 100 in the world. As I would later learn, the shop's individuality in selling Power Rangers paraphernalia to my neighborhood effectively gave it a monopoly over the product, and thus allowed it to inflate its price at will. To my younger, naïve self, that didn't matter; I was ready to spend whatever was necessary to make sure I obtained this collector's item. I was just about to squander all of my saved-up money and fulfill my desire when a friend told me about a company called eBay. From that moment my life changed forever.

My eyes were opened when I first logged on to eBay. I found millions of items being sold at the same time from places all over the world. I was simply amazed by the potential that was available for both buyers and sellers. Although I knew that there were a lot of items being traded, I didn't expect to find such rare commodities as phosphorescent action figures suspended in glass bowls. With little hope in my heart, I sought out the elusive snow globe. Much to my surprise, my search turned up one result. A man in California was selling the exact item I yearned for, and the opening bid was at the quarter of the price that it was being sold for in the local store! I can't even express in words the ecstasy that I felt. I immediately began to bid on the item, not wanting to waste a second. I was pitted against "Bidder 2" in a battle of wits (not to mention modem speed and wallet size), and he proved to be a worthy opponent. With 10 seconds to go I put in my final bid, hoping that I would "seal the deal." Sure enough 10 seconds later, eBay informed me that I had won my first auction. "Bidder 2" was history and I was the new owner of the snow globe, and for half the price that I was originally willing to buy it for. A week later my longing came to an end; the missing, blizzardy piece of my heart arrived in the mail. And though the pleasure of owning a Power Rangers snow globe only lasted a fleeting few months, the intrigue for business that eBay had sparked in me continues to blaze today.

Of course, making purchases through eBay wasn't always easy. As my faith in the company grew after my initial success, eBay became my primary source of acquiring whatever I needed. I found myself buying things all the time at discounted rates and was thrilled with the amount of money I was saving. There was one time, however, when things didn't go quite as planned. My old cell phone had died, and I wanted to replace it with a new one. I searched for a specific model on eBay and specified that I wanted an unused item. When I found a listing at the right price, I immediately bought the phone. When the package arrived a few days later disappointment pierced my heart like a dart on a bull's eye. The cell phone arrived used; it was scratched and dirty and not worth the money I spent. For the first time, eBay had failed me. I immediately sprung into action: I contacted the seller, but he claimed that he had sent a brand new phone. I then contacted eBay and told them of the fraud. Within a few days eBay refunded my money at no cost, and my broken heart completely healed.

I have learned from my mistake. After the heart-shattering incident, I promised myself I would research every item and seller before buying anything, and that when I sell anything, I would make sure the transaction is fair for both the buyer and me. I now make the extra effort to explain the conditions of the items I have for sale with great detail to each and every buyer to prevent unwanted surprises and to make sure nobody feels uncomfortable at any stage of the sale. The value of my new attitude has been recently evidenced by my eBay status promotion to Power-Seller (a title granted to those who sell a significant amount of items as well as have high feedback ratings).

At (college name), I hope to continue learning the intricacies of business and commerce I have gleaned from my experience on eBay, with the ultimate goal of helping to make the world a more efficient place. I feel that furthering my education will help me in my goal of creating my own successful business. Keeping my personal experience as a disappointed consumer in mind, I particularly hope to be able to fully understand how to run the finances of a business, while still keeping customers happy. I believe that only (college name) can supply me with the knowledge and skill to achieve my goal: to be able to supply everyone, on their own terms, with their factory-sealed cell phones and Power Rangers snow globes.

Personal Statement #4 Critique

Personal Statement #4 is an experiential essay, which cleverly captures the student's passion for buying and selling on eBay. The student developed an interest in business early on, and his interest grew through a business venture. By relating a personal experience, the reader becomes interested in the story, yet the focus remains on the actions and decisions made by the student. It is a personal story and it gives you insight into the student's entrepreneurial spirit, which is perfect for a business school. It is a growth experience, where he learned something important from making a mistake. The opening is attention grabbing, and the writer connects the ending to the opening line. It is a well-written and passionate essay. Not everyone may like the concept of the Power Rangers, but that is not the intent of the essay. The excitement of a 17 year old comes shining through.

Evaluating Your Essay

Reading other people's essays can give you an indication of what makes an effective essay. Just remember that essays are subjective, so what one reader really likes, another reader may not like at all. Your essay should be original and it can be on any topic you choose as long as it answers the essay question. The personal statement should honestly reflect who you are and what you're thinking. Writing essays gives you the opportunity to tell admissions counselors something about you that is not clear from the rest of the application. It is a chance for you to advocate for yourself. The checklist below can help you evaluate your personal statement and other essays you write for your college application.

Rating Scale:

☺ = Needs work

☺☺ = I did an okay job

☺☺☺ = I did a very good job

☺☺☺☺ = I did an outstanding job

Essay Checklist	
Criteria	*Evaluation* ☺–☺☺☺☺
Is your opening sentence attention-grabbing?	
Did you show, not tell?	
Did you use descriptive words and give vivid details?	
Did you edit, revise, and proofread?	
Does the essay convey your experiences, impressions, and beliefs?	
Did you answer the question?	
Have you kept the reader in mind?	
Did you use a 17-year-old voice?	
Did you show your essay to a few select people?	
Do you have a clear interest or passion?	
Did you write from the heart?	
Is your essay well written?	
What are the overall impressions of your essay?	

Packaging Yourself:
Application Nuts and Bolts

Apply on time, not at the last minute. And it's important for the student to fill out the application themselves. Parents can prod them to get their applications filed, but it should not be the parent who is doing all the leg work here. Students should answer essay or other questions completely, and if there is something they want the college to know, they should find a way to tell them. Providing the best information possible to the admissions committee is the best way to get the right decision.

–Joan Isaac Mohr, VP and Dean of Admissions, Quinnipiac University

A college application is the culmination of all of the work you have completed in high school so far. It is a way for you to present your case to admissions officers and for them to view your work as a whole. When done correctly and completely, the application represents who you are as a person.

There are many parts to an application, and this chapter discusses the various parts of the application, different types of applications, and what makes an effective application.

What are the elements of a college application?

Your application consists of many components, which should convey a clear and uniform message about who you are and your potential plans. Each element should be carefully developed to form a meaningful and complete package.

- **Personal history:** List where you live, your contact numbers and e-mail address, and information about your family and their educational background (used for statistical purposes).

- **Future plans:** Indicate how you are applying (early action, early decision, or regular decision), whether you are applying for financial aid, and your possible major and career plans.

- **Academic history:** Include information about what high school(s) you have attended and your senior year courses.

- **Test scores:** List your SAT/ACT (discussed in Chapter 2) test score dates and scores (see the section in this chapter about new score reporting policies) and, in some cases, your AP/IB (discussed in Chapter 2) scores. (This information is requested on the Universal College Application [UCA, which is discussed later in this chapter] and on the applications of the most highly selective colleges.) Official test scores must be sent by you from College Board or ACT.

- **Honors, extracurricular activities, and work experience:** Complete this information on the actual application, and you can also usually submit a separate resume containing all of the information about your extracurricular activities, honors/awards, and work/summer experiences.

- **Essays:** This section contains your short answer essays and your personal statement. You can cut and paste your answers or you can attach or upload your essays for online applications. You can attach separate typed sheets with your essays for paper applications.

- **Multimedia information:** The multimedia section is part of the UCA and provides links to additional media you may want to provide, including a video, a portfolio, newspaper articles, etc.

- **Additional information:** Utilize this section to mention anything you want admissions officers to know, including any extenuating circumstances, attendance at a dual curriculum school, explanations for variations in grades, uploaded resumes, personal illness, and other items.

- **Disciplinary information:** Indicate whether you have been suspended, removed, dismissed, or expelled from school, and whether you have had any convictions. If you answer yes to any of these questions, you will be asked to provide an explanation. Your school counselor will also be asked to answer these questions on the "School Report." If you have had some type of infraction, you should discuss how to answer this question with your family and your guidance counselor. Do not hide any information, as your admission can be revoked if it is determined your application is not truthful and accurate.

- **Signature:** Sign (paper applications) or electronically sign (online applications) your application in this section. When you sign, you are agreeing the information contained on the application is accurate and true. You should carefully review your application and make sure everything is accurate before you sign your name.

- **Supplement:** If you are using the Common Application (Common App) or the UCA, check whether the colleges you are applying to have a supplement. When you log in to your account, you can easily see if a college-specific supplement is required. A supplement may contain information about majors, admission deadlines (early or regular), and additional essays.

- **School report:** Completed by your guidance counselor. You may be asked to sign your name and state whether you want to waive your rights to access your counselor and teacher evaluations and other information about you. The Family Education Rights and Privacy Act (FERPA) grants you access to your evaluations and other information, unless the college you will be attending doesn't save the letters or you waive your rights. Check with your guidance counselor about how you should answer this question. Many teachers and counselors do not want students to read their letters, although some may share their letter with you if you ask. Other information on the school report includes your grade point average (GPA), the highest GPA in the class, your test scores, a rating scale of your academic and personal qualities, and an evaluation or letter of recommendation.

- **Teacher recommendation(s):** In some schools, teachers actually complete this form, and in other schools, the teachers' letters are just attached to the form. Check with your high school to find out what the policy is at your school. Colleges don't usually have a problem if the form is not filled out. Again, you may be asked to sign this form and to indicate whether you waive your right to see teachers' letters and ratings.

- **Arts, home school, and athletic supplements:** Complete these forms if you are submitting additional materials, are applying as an athlete, or have been home schooled.

- **Transcript:** You send an official transcript (with an official signature and seal) to every college to which you apply. Some high schools send your application package for you, other schools require you to send the application. Check with your high school for specific instructions.

- **School profile:** Your high school sends a school profile to the colleges to which you are applying. The school profile contains information about your high school, including courses offered, the number of students in the senior class, distribution of grades and/or SAT/ACT scores, percent of students attending four-year colleges, class rank (if used), and other vital information about your high school which helps colleges understand your application.

- **Midyear report:** A midyear report is a form on the Common App and the UCA, but is not required by every college. Some colleges have their own midyear reports, which is part of the application. This report contains updated information about your GPA, your first senior grades, and sometimes an updated evaluation of your progress in your senior year. You are responsible for determining which colleges require this form and then submitting a signed form to your counselor.

- **Final report:** A final report is another form which is part of the Common App and the UCA; some colleges have their own forms. It is very similar to the midyear report, but this report is sent only to the one college you will be attending. A final transcript usually accompanies this form and then your senior year grades are reviewed.

How do I answer optional questions or essays?

Not all of the information requested on college applications is required. One of the most common questions asked is, "To what other colleges are you applying?" or some form of "Where are we ranked on your list of colleges?" Some counselors believe this question should not be answered at all, because it might be used against you. Based on the colleges you list for this question, a college could assume their college is not your first choice, and they may assume you would not accept their offer if you were accepted. Colleges—especially competitive ones—want many of the students to whom they offer admission to accept, driving up their yield rate, thereby affecting their college rankings. The best advice is to list a few colleges in the same tier as the college you are applying to, or don't answer the question at all. The governing body of admissions counselors, NACAC, has revised its recommended practices on this subject, so this question could disappear from college applications.

Other optional questions include marital status, ethnicity, place of birth, and veteran status. It is your choice if you want to answer these questions. Some of the information is for statistical purposes. If you don't think answering these questions will help you in any way, you will not be at a disadvantage if you decide not to answer.

Some colleges have optional essays, which you should answer so admissions counselors can obtain even more information about you. Many applications also contain an "additional information" section, where you can include information not directly asked on the rest of the application, which you want admissions counselors to take into account when reviewing your application.

How do I view and send my scores?

Most colleges want you to send official test scores from the testing organization, College Board, or ACT. When you register for tests in your junior year, you will create an account at www.collegeboard.com or www.act.org. Once an account is created, you will be able to register for a test, view your scores after the test, and send your scores to colleges. Test scores are usually available about 2½ weeks after you take the test, although there is usually a portion of the scores which are not available until later. You can check your scores online or you can wait for a paper copy of your scores. Your high school also receives your test scores. Some high schools place your SAT/ACT scores on your transcript and others don't.

> **Warning:** Many students forget to release their test scores. Know that colleges will not review your application until your file is complete.

If you send your scores to colleges when you register for a test, the first few score reports are free; a fee is charged for more than four score reports, as well as if you release your scores after a certain amount of time after the test. Releasing scores is a priority, so don't forget this important step!

What is the policy on releasing scores?

The ACT policy remains unchanged and it is clear on releasing test scores to colleges. Students must request their scores be sent from a particular test date. If you take the ACT in April and June, you must request your scores be sent for April and then separately for June. You can usually choose which scores to release. However, keep in mind some colleges require you to submit *all* ACT scores, so it is vital you carefully read each college's score reporting policies.

The College Board has a new policy for SATs. Called *Score Choice*, this policy went into effect with the March 2009 SAT administration. Score Choice says students can choose which *administration* of the SAT Reasoning test they wish to report, and which *individual* SAT subject tests they wish to report. If you take the Chemistry, Math 1, and Literature subject tests in one sitting, you can elect to release none, one, two, or all three of these scores once you see them. If you take the SAT Reasoning test in March or June, you can decide not to release your entire set of March SAT scores if you are not happy with the scores.

The problem with Score Choice is that guidance and admissions counselors believe this policy favors wealthier students, who could conceivably take the SAT five times and only release scores from two of the five test administrations. Also, most colleges take the highest Critical Reading, Math, and Writing scores anyway, and colleges want to see the historical progression of your test scores.

Although the intent of the policy is to reduce student stress, it actually adds stress to the process. Students have to think strategically about which scores to release, and some colleges may not accept this policy. Some colleges, including Harvard and the University of Chicago, have said they will honor the Score Choice policy. Other colleges have said they will not honor this policy, and they want to see all scores from all test administrations. These colleges include Yale, Pomona, Columbia, Cornell, University of Southern California, Stanford, University of Pennsylvania, and Claremont McKenna. As of this writing, colleges were still formulating their Score Choice policy, so check with your guidance counselor or look at each college's Web site.

According to the College Board, there is no charge for using Score Choice. You have to choose the Score Choice option when you release scores. The default option is when you release your scores, all previous scores are sent. The best course of action is to check each college's Web site or check with an admission officer regarding how each college is treating this policy. It is also a good idea to check with your guidance counselor before releasing test scores.

Do I need to submit supplementary materials?

If you are planning to attend college for a creative or artistic field, you are usually required to submit supplementary materials in your chosen field. Admission must be gained through the admissions office based on grades, standardized test scores (if required), and other factors, and you must also be admitted based on your artistic talent. If you are interested in music, musical theatre, drama, acting, or dance, you have to attend an audition, where your potential ability in that field will be assessed. Check with each school in which you are interested for individual requirements and deadlines for scheduling auditions.

If you are interested in art, film, architecture, or creative or dramatic writing, you need to submit supplementary materials in the form of a portfolio. If you are planning to study interior design, graphic design, fashion design, illustration, photography, and other areas of art, specific portfolios may be necessary.

If you take art in high school, you can work with your art teacher or an art professional to develop your portfolio. You may be charged a fee for the portfolio you are developing. Requirements vary from college to college regarding whether you need to submit original artwork, slides, or CDs, size limits, media used, and deadlines. Portfolios usually contain three elements:

- 🎓 **Observational art:** Pieces that demonstrate your drawing ability
- 🎓 **Personal art:** Sketches and pieces done informally, not in a class setting
- 🎓 **Home tests:** You have a short period of time to complete specific pieces, depending on your major

Whether you submit original art, slides, or CDs, a typed summary list describing all of your submitted pieces must be included. You need to list the title of the selection, the date it was completed, the size, and the media (charcoal, watercolor, sculpture, etc.) used.

Because there are additional materials required, the deadlines for art schools are usually later than those for liberal arts and other types of colleges. To help you prepare your portfolio, you can work with your art teacher or you can take a portfolio development or preparation course or a continuing education course for a fee at a local college, or attend a pre-college summer program at a local museum or art school.

There are two organizations which give you feedback during the portfolio development process:

- 🎓 National Portfolio Day Association (NPDA)
- 🎓 NACAC Performing and Visual Arts (PVA) college fairs

The National Portfolio Day Association began in 1978 to give students an opportunity to have their work reviewed by professionals representing accredited schools by the National Association of Schools of Art and Design. These events, held September to January, are held at colleges and art schools throughout the country. You do not need to register in advance, and there is no charge for these events. For a current calendar, visit www.portfolioday.net.

The Performing and Visual Art College Fairs, sponsored by NACAC, are for students interested in pursuing majors in art, dance, music, theater, and related areas. At these fairs held in September to November in cities all over the country, you can meet with admissions counselors to discuss portfolios, auditions, and admissions requirements. You can view the current year's schedule at www.nacacnet.org/EventsTraining/CollegeFairs/pva/Pages/default.aspx.

By submitting supplementary materials, you are giving admissions officers another piece of the puzzle about you as an applicant. It is suggested you attend one of these national events, or you can attend a portfolio review by individual colleges you are applying to when they are offered.

Are there ways to expedite the application process?

There are many details that accompany the application process. You should follow the procedures outlined by your high school's guidance office, as there is tremendous variation in how high schools process applications. In some schools, the counseling office is responsible for reviewing and mailing out applications, mailing each student's applications separately or as a batch to each college. Other high schools ask students to mail their own applications and the guidance office sends in transcripts, letters of recommendations, and the school profile.

> **TIP:** Many high school guidance offices communicate with their students via e-mail, the school's Web site, mailings home, or notices posted in the guidance office. Be alert and read everything; it is your responsibility to read these communications from your guidance office as they contain critical information and deadlines about the admissions process.

Applications may be due to your guidance office two to four weeks before the actual application deadline, giving counselors enough time to pull all of the materials together.

Some suggestions for making the process more efficient are as follows:

- Get organized. Use folders or an accordion folder to keep copies of all correspondence with colleges, confirmations of campus tours, hotel confirmations, copies of applications, and other materials for each college.

- Check that your e-mail address is user friendly. If there is any doubt, create an e-mail address that you will use specifically for college applications, and check your e-mail frequently.

- If you are under 18, verify whether the application requires a parent's signature in addition to your own; this may vary from application to application.

- Do not ask teachers for letters of recommendations at the last minute. Give them plenty of time to complete your letter and, if appropriate, give them pre-addressed stamped envelopes to mail letters to the colleges. Inform teachers whether you want them to send letters directly to the college or give them to the guidance office.

- Check that you have indicated whether you waive your right to see letters and other information contained on your application.

Should you give your Social Security number?

With the growing concern over identity theft, many colleges are moving away from requiring Social Security numbers. If you have any concerns, check the application; as long as it is not required, you do not need to submit your Social Security number. Ask the college if they can use your date of birth instead of your Social Security number. It is not uncommon for a large university to have several students with the same name, so use your middle name or initial and your date of birth to distinguish you from other applicants.

- Keep copies of your application, especially your essays and resume. Print hard copies in case your computer crashes and these documents are not retrievable. Save the information on a flash drive to protect and save the data on the application.

- Jot down your user name and password when applying online. Try to use the same user name and password for all your college applications, so it's unlikely you'll forget them. I've seen many students panic when they realize they can't access their accounts. Much time can be wasted trying to retrieve this information.

- If you are not applying online, your application should be neat with no cross-outs. (The use of correction fluid is okay.) It should be neatly handwritten or typed. Make a copy of the original first, and when it is perfect, you can use the original paper application. Most paper applications can be downloaded, so you can reprint them as necessary.

- Print and submit all required forms to your counselor, including the school report, teacher recommendation form, and midyear report.

Application Tips from Experts

"Be yourself. Authenticity is important. We want to get to know each applicant—a real, live human being—from a piece of paper. Anything you can do to add personality, to make your application 'come alive' helps us get to know you and make a good decision."–Lorne Robinson, Dean of Admissions and Financial Aid, Macalester College

"Make an authentic presentation. Rather than trying to figure out what the college wants to hear, spend time thinking about how to tell your story in ways that reflect who you are and what you will be offering the college. Good writing always gets the attention of admissions counselors at selective colleges. Remember to proofread to minimize careless mechanical errors."–Paul Marthers, EdD, Dean of Admission, Reed College

"Do your homework! Make sure you have researched the college to ensure that it is a good academic fit prior to applying. In addition, follow our directions. We take time to put together an admissions process, and it makes a difference when students respect that process and do their best to follow it."–Jacquelyn Nealon, Vice President Enrollment Services, New York Institute of Technology

Application Checklist

ITEM	YES	NO	NOTES
Did I jot down my user name and password?			
Did I sign my application?			

ITEM	YES	NO	NOTES
Did a parent sign my application (if necessary)?			
Is my e-mail address user friendly?			
Did I ask my teachers for letters of recommendations?			
Do I know when my applications are due?			
Did I print all of the required forms?			
Did I make a copy of my application?			
Did I submit everything on time?			
Now that my application is complete, do I have a way to organize all of my information?			
Did I send my SAT/ACT scores to all of the colleges on my list?			

How do I design a brag sheet/résumé?

The brag sheet/résumé/extracurricular activities list is a way to compile all of your activities to demonstrate your interests and leadership skills. A résumé should be between one and three pages. It highlights the clubs, organizations, work and summer experiences, and community service in which you participated. You can also list any honors or awards, including honor societies, sports awards such as Most Valuable Player (MVP) or Most Improved Player (MIP), subject awards, participation in contests or competitions, and other accomplishments.

TIP: Some colleges verify activities which students list on their brag sheets, so don't be tempted to exaggerate your accomplishments.

The résumé should be an honest reflection of all of your activities inside and outside of school since ninth grade. It can include activities you plan to continue or pursue in twelfth grade. Your résumé needs to show a progression of activities and a demonstrated passion for one or two areas, such as science, math, community service, leadership, music, writing, etc. If you can do so, you may want to present a unifying theme tying together many of your activities so your participation in an activity or club makes sense. So for example, if you have a passion for science, being a judge in a middle school science fair, entering science competitions, founding a science research club in your school, and tutoring peers in science are all linked in some way. If you don't have a clear passion or interest in something, that's okay.

Some colleges want you to list your activities in order of their importance to you, and others leave the order up to you. You can list your activities in chronological order or you can start with activities in which you had a leadership role. Take the same care in preparing a résumé that you would in completing your essay and the rest of your application. A well-designed résumé can give admissions counselors a clear window into who you are and what you care about.

Tips for Creating a Brag Sheet

"Students help themselves most when they send a concise and comprehensive list of chief activities, passions, and accomplishments. List the activities in order of depth of commitment and importance to you. Do not inflate your level of involvement. Do not join clubs just to have another listing on the brag sheet/résumé. Admissions officers can always see through that strategy."–Paul Marthers, EdD, Dean of Admissions, Reed College

"We look to see what the student has added to their high school experience. We'd rather see a 'short' list of activities that the student has enjoyed in depth, rather than a 'long' list of activities that the student has only just joined in the junior/senior year likely to beef up their application to college. Are they a leader, do they work well with group projects, have they given of their time (other than what's required by the school) to do something for others? A student who has had to work to help support their family may not have a long list of activities, but the work they've been doing shows that they can shoulder responsibility, can learn new skills, and can work to the best of their ability at whatever that job entails. That can be just as important as the list of clubs or sports that many applicants can talk about. If a student has not found activities of interest to them in their school surroundings, they can tell us about their community or religious activities such as scouting or volunteer groups."–Joan Isaac Mohr, VP and Dean of Admissions, Quinnipiac University

"I'm looking for evidence that the student is capable of handling more than just the work in the classroom. Students who demonstrate the ability to lead, motivate, and juggle multiple responsibilities are likely to become active, contributing members of our college community. The key is not to have a laundry list of items on a résumé, but rather fewer, higher quality experiences that speak to a student's character and leadership."–Jacquelyn Nealon, VP Enrollment Services, New York Institute of Technology

What should my brag sheet look like?

The formats for an activities sheet on the Common App, the UCA, and a college's own application vary slightly, but the information contained on all of them is pretty similar. You need to list the activity (club or organization), the grade level (9, 10, 11, 12), the number of hours per week, positions held, honors or awards received, and on some forms whether you will participate in this activity in college.

You can estimate the number of hours per week as best as possible. You should be accurate in your information, especially in leadership positions. Some applications instruct you to submit information in the extracurricular activities section of the application, even if you intend to attach a separate résumé. You can have separate sections for honors/awards and work/summer experiences. Do not list abbreviations or acronyms (i.e., P.A.S.T. club), which someone from outside your school may not know. Describe any organizations/activities which are not self-explanatory.

If you are planning to pursue a business-related degree, you may want to attach a traditional résumé format (see third sample brag sheet) as it looks more professional and business oriented. Some examples of brag sheets follow on the next several pages.

ILANA R. PICASSO

EXTRACURRICULAR ACTIVITIES, PAGE 1 OF 2

ACTIVITY	GRADES PARTICIPATED	DESCRIPTION	APPROX. HRS/WK	POSITIONS HELD
Yearbook	12	Supervise students on the art committee, select and create artwork	2 hrs/wk	Art Editor
Drama Club	10–12	Create artwork for plays using various media, supervise construction of scenery and backdrops	10 hrs/wk from November–April	Art Director
Art Club	9–12	Recruit new members, coordinate fundraising, plan events, and run meetings	1 hr/wk	President (12) Member (9–11)
Art Academy	11–12	Assist children with art projects after school, prepare and clean art supplies	2 hrs/wk	Instructor
Volleyball Team	10–12	Member of junior varsity and varsity teams	1 hr/wk	Member
Artistic Designs	Summer 2008	Interned with art director, assisted in creating layouts for advertising company	30 hrs/wk	Intern

ILANA R. PICASSO

EXTRACURRICULAR ACTIVITIES PAGE 2 OF 2

AWARDS/HONORS	*GRADES*
First place in Art Teachers' Association poster contest	11
Honorable Mention in statewide art contest	11
Cover art selected for local publication	11
Artwork selected for display in local museum	11
Most Valuable Player: Volleyball	11
National Honor Society	11
National Spanish Honor Society	10–11

KIMBERLY I. KENNEDY
EXTRACURRICULAR ACTIVITIES

Activity	Grades	Approx. hrs/wk	Position/Honors	Participate in College
Mock Trial	9–12	3 hrs/wk	Captain (11–12)	Yes
Current Events Club	11–12	1 hr/wk	Founder	No
Model Congresses	11–12	NA	Delegate	Yes
Anti-Bullying Program	10–12	2 hrs/wk	Presenter	No
Blood Drive	9–12	NA	Coordinator (12); Participant (9–11)	Yes
Key Club	9–12	2 hrs/wk	Vice President (12); Member (9–11)	Yes
Judge Potter	Summer 2008	25 hrs/wk	Intern	Yes
Leg. Sam Cooke	Summer 2007	25 hrs/wk	Campaign Volunteer	No
Camp ABC	Summer 2006	40 hrs/wk	Counselor	Yes/No

HONORS/AWARDS
Regional Winners Mock Trial Team–2008

AP Scholar

Spanish National Honor Society

National Honor Society

MARISSA L. TRUMP
PAGE 1 OF 2

123 College Avenue   Home: 123-345-6789
Anywhere, US 11234   Cell: 123-345-6788

EXTRACURRICULAR ACTIVITIES
Stock Market Team, Captain   September 2005–June 2009
Led team to third place finish statewide

Business Manager, Yearbook   September 2008–June 2009
Raised $20,000 in ads to cover costs of Yearbook

Fundraising Chair, Local Charity   September 2008–June 2009
Led committee which raised $5,000 for Breast Cancer

Math Team, Member   September 2006–June 2009
Traveled with math team to competitions
Our team placed 1st two years in a row

College Bowl Team, Member   September 2006–June 2009
Junior Varsity and Varsity member

Math Tutor   September 2006–June 2009
Tutored peers in algebra, geometry, pre-calculus, and calculus

WORK EXPERIENCE
eBay Business   September 2007–June 2009
Buy/sell comic books, made profit of $3,750

ABC Hedgefund Intern   Summer 2008
Shadowed Hedgefund manager

ABC Camp Counselor   Summers 2006 and 2007
Responsible for 5th-grade boys

MARISSA L. TRUMP
PAGE 2 OF 2

HONORS/AWARDS

Top 3 in school in American Mathematics Competition   12th Grade

Top 10 in county math competition   11th Grade

Bronze medal in local college math fair   11th Grade

AP Scholar   11th Grade

Math award   10th Grade

EDUCATION

Abraham Lincoln High School   September 2005–June 2009

INTERESTS

eBay, stock market, trivia, sports, Scrabble

Should I apply online?

Applying online is a popular and usually easier way to apply to colleges. According to the National Association of College Admissions Counselors (NACAC), colleges received approximately 70 percent of all applications online in 2007, and it is a growing trend. It is fairly easy to type in your information, especially the statistical information about you and your family. On some online applications, you may have trouble cutting and pasting your essay or uploading your essay if it is too long, so you may have to edit the essay and make it shorter.

Complete the application at least one to two weeks before the deadline to ensure you have no difficulty in completing and submitting your application. Also, make sure you actually hit the "submit" button. You may think you have applied online, but some students don't submit the application properly. You should get some type of confirmation, either at the time you apply or in a separate e-mail. Print these confirmations and keep them in the folders you have for each college.

> **TIP:** If you wait until the last minute to apply, some Web sites crash from heavy volume and you may be unable to complete your application close to the deadline.

Applying online gives your application a nice, neat appearance. On some Web sites, you can upload your brag sheet as you develop it; on others you have to follow the format you are given. You may be able to include only your top seven activities. If you want to add more activities to your brag sheet, you may be able to send a separate résumé by paper along with your other documents (transcript, letters of recommendation), or you can upload your résumé in the "additional information" section of the application. Some high schools electronically send transcripts and letters, and others send these documents by paper.

It is extremely important to inform your guidance counselor that you have applied online. Some students forget to tell their counselors they have applied online, so their documents are not sent. Your guidance office may have a form for you to complete, listing all of the schools you've applied to online, so check with your counselor. If you apply online, you can pay by credit card when you submit your application or you can sometimes send a check separately. Either way, don't forget to pay your application fee or request a fee waiver if needed from your counselor.

If you prefer, you can usually generate an application online and then print it and mail it so everything is typed. Do not also submit it online; colleges will not accept two versions of the same application, one on paper and one online, so choose which way you want to apply. Also, many colleges do not want you to mix and match online and paper applications, so you can't generally do the Common App online and then do the supplement on paper. Read the instructions on the college's Web site, the Common App Web site, or the UCA Web site. Paper applications are still being used, but always check with the college to which you are applying.

Should I Use the Common Application or the Universal College Application?

There are two types of applications, the Common App and the UCA, which can be used to streamline the application process. They are growing in popularity, and more colleges are becoming members of these organizations each year.

Common Application

The Common App is a not-for-profit organization, in existence for over 30 years, which provides students with an opportunity to apply to over 350 colleges and universities. According to the Common App Web site, about 400,000 students applied online and submitted about 1.4 million applications. Additionally, many students also submitted applications using the paper Common App. The colleges that accept the Common App have agreed to review applications through a holistic approach, using objective and subjective admissions factors (reviewed in Chapter 2).

> To apply via the Common App, go to their Web site www.commonapp.org. (Make sure to use two *p*s in *app* or you will be directed to a different Web site.)

If you are using the Common App, there is a very useful "Requirements Grid," which is accessible on the "Download Forms" drop-down menu. It contains:

- A listing of the member colleges and universities
- Deadline information
- Application fees
- Whether a supplement is required
- Which standardized tests are required (if any)
- Which school forms are required

Note: While the original purpose of the Common App was to streamline the college application to make it easier to apply, many colleges still require their own supplements, which can be very time consuming.

Universal College Application (UCA)

The UCA was developed in 2007 by ApplicationsOnline,LLC, and was ready for use in fall 2008. Over 80 colleges participate in the UCA. The application is very similar to the Common App. The UCA aims to be more inclusive in terms of its participating colleges and the applicants who apply. To become a member college of the UCA, colleges and universities must abide by the National Association of College Admissions Counselors' (NACAC) policies.

> To apply via the UCA, go to their Web site: www.universalcollegeapp.com.

The UCA features a very useful spreadsheet called "UCA College Requirements: First Year Applicants." It contains the following data:

- Information about early action, early decision, and regular decision deadlines for each member college
- A link to each college's supplement, if required
- Information about other school forms that are required, including the school report, midyear reports, and final reports

You can apply using either of these applications, as long as the colleges you are interested in participate in these applications.

How Do I Solve Common Problems on These Applications?

Technical difficulties can arise when using any online application. Web sites can crash, especially close to deadlines, and other difficulties may occur. Both the Common App and the UCA have a section for common technical problems (Frequently Asked Questions) with troubleshooting steps you can take to correct the problem. You can also contact Technical Support for both application Web sites; just allow yourself several days to obtain a reply and fix the problem.

Two common questions that arise when using the Common App involve creating alternate forms of the application and applying Early Decision II after you have applied to an Early Decision school and were deferred or rejected.

Creating Alternate Forms

In order to create different versions in order to change information from one application to another (e.g., different majors), you can take the following steps:

1. Submit one version of the Common App, then log out.
2. Go to https://app.commonapp.org/Application/ApplicantLogin.aspx?allowcopy=true.
3. Enter your user name and password on the login screen and click "login."
4. When the Common App screen pops up, click on the "Replicate" link to create a different version and make any changes necessary to your applications. A new version with a drop-down window appears giving you access to your applications.

Applying Early Decision II

The Common App only lets you apply Early Decision to one school, so if you want to apply to an Early Decision II (second chance early decision) school after you were not accepted to an Early Decision school, Common App suggests the following steps:

1. Choose "Regular Decision" on the Common App.
2. Choose "Early Decision II" on the college's supplement.

What is a priority application?

A *priority application,* also known as a blue ribbon or freebie application, differs from other applications in that a college invites you to apply, usually with no application fee and within a certain deadline. You may have been invited to apply because you demonstrated your interest in applying by visiting a college's Web site or by requesting information from them. Priority applications are usually streamlined, with some of the information already completed. In addition to not paying a fee, you may be waived from writing an essay or submitting letters of recommendation.

> **WARNING:** Some colleges use priority applications to encourage you to apply just so they can reject you, which can improve their college rankings. It can be a cruel method, because students become excited and feel good about themselves. I know of one student who received one of these applications from a college which was out of his range. He insisted the college must want him to attend, so he filled out the application free of charge, and then he was rejected as anticipated.

The purpose of priority applications is to entice students to apply. It appears you are going to be accepted to a college issuing one of these applications, but there is actually no guarantee of acceptance.

If you receive a priority application, do not automatically complete one. Look at the college's Web site and determine if the college is a possible option for you. If it looks feasible, you can take a chance and apply as long as you won't be too upset if you are not admitted.

What is a QuestBridge application?

QuestBridge is a nonprofit matching service that partners high-achieving, low-income students with some of the most competitive colleges in the nation. If you meet the selection criteria and if you are selected as a QuestBridge Scholar, you receive a full scholarship to the participating college if you are accepted for admission. The QuestBridge scholarship is available as an online application only at www.questbridge.org.

The application is longer and more involved than other college applications, and the deadline for completing the application and all other documentation is the end of September of your senior year. Income information is required to determine if you are within the income restrictions. In the 2007 application process, approximately 900 students received $90 million in financial aid (no loans).

If you qualify to use the application, you can apply to the partner colleges for free. For all of the rules and regulations, go to their Web site. Information about other ways to obtain money for college is contained in Chapter 7.

QUESTBRIDGE PARTNER COLLEGES

Amherst	Claremont McKenna
Bowdoin	Columbia
California Institute of Technology	Emory
University of Chicago	Haverford

Massachusetts Institute of Technology	Scripps
Northwestern	Stanford
University of Notre Dame	Swarthmore
Oberlin	Trinity
Parsons School of Design	Vassar
University of Pennsylvania	Wellesley
Pomona	Wesleyan
Princeton	Williams
Rice	Yale

How do I know if my application was received?

One of the most stressful parts of the application process is wondering if your application was received on time and whether it is complete. Whatever you do, don't panic! It is very common to receive an e-mail or letter from a college saying your application can't be reviewed because items are missing from your application. If you can, try to visualize the mail room of a large university filled with 30,000 or more applications with hardworking people trying to match your SAT/ACT scores, transcripts, letters of recommendation, and other documents into the correct file. Also keep in mind that it can take several weeks to process your application, and in the meantime you may receive one of these "your file is incomplete" letters.

Your guidance office usually keeps records of when your application (if it is on paper) and the documents are mailed to colleges. If you are responsible for submitting your application, keep copies and good records of when documents were sent and when SAT/ACT scores were released. Do not blame your guidance office if there is a problem, but ask them in a calm manner to double-check when your application was sent. It is not uncommon for guidance departments to send two or three transcripts for one student, if the transcripts were lost, misplaced, or filed incorrectly.

It is your responsibility to check with each admissions office to confirm that your file is complete. You can call the admissions office and ask if your file is complete. If it is not complete, you can still send in documents after the official deadline has passed, especially if you are notified by a college about missing documents. Do not ignore any e-mail messages or other communications from colleges about your application. With the increase in online applications, it is vital to notify your guidance counselor that you have submitted applications online, so the counselor can send the appropriate documents. You can also follow up to make sure that your teachers have written their letters of recommendation. Many colleges confirm that your application has been received, so check your e-mail and online accounts frequently for updated messages.

> Do not take anything for granted during the admissions process, and remember it is ultimately your responsibility to check with your guidance counselor and the admissions office that everything regarding your application is complete. The Tracking Applications Checklist on the following page can help you with this process.

Tracking Applications Checklist					
ITEM	YES	DATE	NO	FOLLOW-UP ACTIONS TAKEN/DATE	NOTES
Did I release my SAT/ACT scores?					
Did College Board and ACT send my scores?					
Did my guidance office send in appropriate documents?					
Did I send in the appropriate documents with the required postage and before the deadline?					
Have I checked with the teachers to verify they have written/ mailed/submitted their letters?					
Was I notified my application was received by a college?					
Did I receive an "incomplete application" letter or e-mail?					
Am I checking my e-mail/online accounts frequently?					
Did I submit supplementary materials, as required?					

Financial Aid 101: How to Pay for College

"My parents make too much money to qualify for financial aid but not enough to afford the university I want to attend."

"The financial aid process is too difficult to understand, so why bother trying?"

"There is so much scholarship money out there; you have to hire a scholarship company to find it."

"Private universities are not affordable for my family, so I shouldn't even consider applying to any."

"Colleges only want the brightest students from middle- and upper-middle-class families."

"I am the first one in my family to go to college; it's a shame there are no resources available to me."

There are many myths and misconceptions about the access, availability, and ease of the financial aid process. Parents of students from low-income families may not understand the process or might believe there are few resources to help them. Parents of students from high-income families may not believe they qualify for financial aid, so they don't bother looking for sources of money for college. None of the above statements are accurate, and by the end of this chapter, you are going to have a better sense of where you can obtain financial aid and what's involved in applying for financial aid. You also receive some tips and techniques from experts in the field.

What are some common misperceptions?

A 2009 nationwide phone survey, conducted by the nonprofit organization Public Agenda, surveyed people's perceptions about financial aid and tabulated the following results:

63 percent think the cost of college is going up at a faster rate than other items.

74 percent believe the price of college should not stop students who are qualified and motivated from going to college.

67 percent feel students have to borrow too much money to pay for college.

57 percent believe financial aid is available to help students pay for college.

NEED-BLIND VERSUS NEED-SENSITIVE ADMISSIONS

Some colleges practice the policy of *need-blind* admissions, while others are *need-sensitive.* Our financial aid experts explain the differences between need-blind and need-sensitive policies.

According to Jacquelyn Nealon, VP Enrollment Services at New York Institute of Technology, schools that are need-blind focus on the academic profile of the student, as well as other contributing factors like leadership. They do not consider a student's ability to pay in the decision-making process about who to admit and they do not require financial information prior to acceptance.

Need-sensitive colleges take into account a student's financial need when reviewing his or her college application.

When researching colleges, you should check whether they are need blind or need sensitive. Regardless of their policy, you should know whether a college will meet your full financial need, what the average financial aid package is, and whether merit- and/or need-based scholarships and grants are available.

> *"Colleges that practice need-blind admissions have no idea how much financial aid is going to be needed on a student-by-student basis and are often unable to meet 100 percent of a student's need as a result. Colleges that are need-sensitive have a financial profile on each potential applicant and they admit students with financial need in mind in order to assure adequate financial aid for their admitted pool of students."*
>
> –Dominic Yoia, Senior Director of Financial Aid at Quinnipiac University

Some Need-Blind and Need-Sensitive Colleges	
NEED-BLIND	**NEED-SENSITIVE/AWARE**
Ivy League colleges	Bates (ME)
Bowdoin (ME)	Bryn Mawr (PA)
Brandeis (MA)	Carleton (MN)
Carnegie Mellon (PA)	Dickinson (PA)
Davidson (NC)	Franklin & Marshall (PA)
Grinnell (IA)	Kenyon (OH)

NEED-BLIND	NEED-SENSITIVE/AWARE
Lehigh (PA)	Muhlenberg (PA)
Middlebury (VT)	Occidental (CA)
New York University (NY)	Pitzer (CA)
Northwestern (IL)	Reed (OR)
Pomona (CA)	Skidmore (PA)
Rice (TX)	Trinity (CT)
Swarthmore (PA)	Union (NY)
University of Chicago (IL)	Wheaton (MA)
University of Rochester (NY)	
University of Southern California (CA)	
Wake Forest (NC)	
Williams (MA)	

According to a 2008 National Association of College Admissions Counselors (NACAC) study on financial aid, only 32 percent of public universities and 18 percent of private universities actually meet the full need of students. Although most universities don't meet 100 percent of students' needs, that doesn't mean you should rule out attending an out-of-state university or a private university. As discussed in Chapter 3, you should review the total costs of

> **TIP:** Transfer students, international students, and students accepted from the waitlist may be exempt from need-blind policies, so check with each college about its policies.

all colleges you are considering after you receive a financial aid package (discussed later in this chapter). Colleges like students who have geographical diversity (students from states other than their own), and an out-of-state university or private university may offer you scholarships or grants.

What are the costs?

Cost, of course, is an important consideration in deciding which college to attend. You are not alone if you and your family are concerned about how to finance your education. The cost of attending college, known as the cost of attendance (COA), consists of:

- **Tuition:** Cost of your classes
- **Fees:** Gym, lab, registration, fraternity, and special program fees such as pharmacy, business, and science programs

- **Room and board:** Housing and meal plans
- **Books and supplies:** Books required for each class plus art supplies, calculators,etc.
- **Personal expenses:** Entertainment, laundry
- **Transportation:** Expenses to and from home, whether commuting or living on campus
- **Miscellaneous expenses:** Clothing, bus fare, cell phone and land line bills

There is a tremendous amount of variation in tuition between and within public and private universities. The most reasonable tuition is usually found in community colleges and city or state university systems, followed by out-of-state universities, and then private universities. In some cases, it could be more financially affordable to attend a public university in a neighboring state. For example, the State University of New York (SUNY) system has very affordable tuition rates for out-of-state students. You may also consider attending one of the well-regarded universities in Canada, where tuition for international students is fairly reasonable. It is also possible to find some real bargains, namely free tuition, at the following universities:

TUITION-FREE COLLEGES

Berea College (KY)

City University of New York Macaulay Honors College

Cooper Union (NY)

Curtis Institute of Music (PA)

Franklin W. Olin College of Engineering (MA)

US Military Academy

US Air Force Academy

US Naval Academy

US Coast Guard Academy

US Merchant Marine Academy

Webb Institute (NY)

The issue of cost naturally enters into your decision as to whether you should apply to a public university or a private university. You might initially think you should avoid private colleges if money is an issue in your family. Consider the sticker price of a car your family wants to buy. Except for certain makes and models, families don't usually pay the full price of a car. The same can be said for the cost of private universities; not everyone pays the full sticker price for college. Private universities may actually have more funds to give to those in need or to those who have outstanding academic ability. Many private universities have endowments through various individuals and organizations, and they use these funds to attract the following types of students:

- Students who are the first in their family to attend college
- Students who are from low-income families
- Students who are academically gifted
- Students who might add to the geographic or ethnic diversity of their student population

Some of the most selective colleges in the country have very generous financial aid packages for those in various income levels. The policies for some of these colleges are outlined below:

Harvard College

- Students of families who have incomes below $60,000 will not have to contribute their income toward tuition, room and board, and mandatory fees.
- Students with families who earn less than $180,000 will pay varying percentages of their income. If a family earns $120,000 to $180,000, they will be asked to pay 10 percent of their income. For families earning $60,000 to $120,000, the families will be expected to contribute no more than 10 percent of their income.
- Harvard has eliminated loans to students receiving financial aid.

Columbia University

- For families with incomes under $60,000, parents do not contribute towards tuition, room, and board.
- For families who earn $60,000 to $100,000, parents pay significantly less than the full sticker price.
- Columbia will meet 100 percent of a student's demonstrated need for four years of college.
- Columbia has eliminated loans to students, replacing them with grants.

Princeton University

- There is a no-loan policy for students with demonstrated financial need.
- Princeton will meet 100 percent of financial need.
- There are reasonable expected contributions for parents and students.
- Full funding is provided for study abroad programs for students with demonstrated need.

Grinnell College

- Grinnell is committed to meeting the full financial need of admitted students.
- Financial aid consists of a campus work opportunity, a loan capped at $2,000 per year, and the rest in grants or scholarship funds.

Rensselaer Polytechnic Institute

- More than 90 percent of Rensselaer students receive scholarship aid.

- All applicants are assigned a financial aid counselor to guide them through need-based funding.

- Rensselaer Medalists are guaranteed $60,000 in scholarships over 4 years.

- Undergraduates can receive an additional year of aid to pursue a master's degree while completing their bachelor's degree through its recently announced co-terminal program.

What financial aid options are available?

In 2007, approximately $82 billion in federal aid alone was awarded to more than 10 million students. Financial aid consists of:

- **Grants:** Gifts from various sources that don't have to be paid back. Sources of grants can be federal, state, or local, or grants can be offered by colleges.

- **Loans:** Loans do need to be paid back with interest. Sources of loans can be federal, state, or private.

- **Scholarships:** Scholarships from various sources do not need to be paid back, and for certain scholarships, an application may be required. Scholarships can be need-based or merit-based; sources include corporations, civic and community clubs and agencies, and federal, state, and local governments.

- **Employment:** Federal work-study programs provide students with part-time jobs on campus. Students also often carry part-time and summer jobs.

GRANTS, LOANS, AND WORK STUDY

The chart below has information about grants, loans, and work-study programs. Scholarship information is discussed in a later section.

GRANTS, LOANS, AND WORK-STUDY PROGRAMS

Program	Description	Eligibility	How to Apply
GRANTS			
Federal Pell Grant	Up to $4,731/year	U.S. citizen or eligible noncitizen with valid Social Security #, high school diploma, financial need required; must register for selective service and have no drug convictions	File FAFSA
Academic Competitiveness Grant (ACG)	Up to $750 1st year; up to $1,300 2nd year	Same as Pell Grant: Must be enrolled full time; must maintain a 3.0 GPA	File FAFSA
National Science & Math Access to Retain Talent Grant (SMART)	Up to $4,000 for 3rd and 4th years	Same as Pell Grant for math, science, technology, engineering or critical foreign language majors	File FAFSA
Teacher Educational Assistance for College & Higher Education Grant (TEACH)	Up to $4,000/year	U.S. citizen or eligible noncitizen in a participating college teacher education program. Must maintain a 3.25 GPA	File FAFSA
Federal Supplemental Educational Opportunity Grants (FSEOG)	Up to $4,000/year	Same as Pell Grant	File FAFSA
Grants from Colleges	Varies	Varies	Check with Financial Aid office at the college or Web site
State Grants	Varies	Varies	Check Web site: wdcrobcolp01.ed.gov/ programs/erod/org_list. cfm?category_cd=sgt

continued

Program	Description	Eligibility	How To Apply
LOANS			
Federal Perkins Loans	Low interest rates, up to $4,000/year, up to 10 years to repay	Same as Pell Grant	File FAFSA
Federal Stafford Loans (Subsidized)	Low interest rates. Government pays interest while student is in school, up to $3,500 1st year, $4,500 2nd year, and $5,500 3rd and 4th years	Demonstrated need, same as Pell Grant; must sign a Master Promissory Note	Master Promissory Note
Federal Stafford Loans (Unsubsidized)	Low interest rates; responsible for required interest payments; amounts vary depending on dependency status and year in school	No financial need, subject to lender approval	File FAFSA and Master Promissory Note
Federal PLUS Loans	Loans for parents; fixed interest rates; can apply for cost of attendance minus financial aid received	No financial need required	Contact Financial Aid office or Lender
Federal Direct Student Loan Program	Alternative loan program, if college participates		File FAFSA, contact Financial Aid office
Private Loans	Varies	Varies	Contact Financial Aid office or Lender
OTHER PROGRAMS			
Federal Work-Study Program	Part-time job on campus	Same as Pell Grant	File FAFSA, contact Financial Aid office

Program	Description	Eligibility	How To Apply
MILITARY/SERVICE PROGRAMS			
ROTC	Up to full tuition and monthly stipend, commitment to serve, requirements vary for Army, Navy, or Air Force	Competitive, review of high school record	Contact high school, local recruitment office, or ROTC at college
Americorps	1 year service program. Up to 2 awards of $4,725	17 years old, citizen, natural or lawful permanent resident	www.americorps.org
Teach for America	2-year commitment to teach in urban/rural areas, $9,450 over 2 years + salary	Bachelor's degree with 2.5 GPA, U.S. citizen/permanent resident alien	www.teachforamerica.org
Peace Corps	2 year commitment, Covered by insurance Transition allowance of $6,000, 15 percent of Perkins loan debt forgiven	18 years. old, U.S. citizen	www.peacecorps.gov

TAX CREDITS AND OTHER PROGRAMS

In addition to grants, scholarships, loans, and work study, there are other methods for assisting you in paying for college:

- Tax credits
- College savings programs
- College credit programs

There are two tax credits available for parents or for students with an independent tax status: The Hope Credit and the Lifetime Learning Credit. The Hope Credit is a tax credit available to eligible families for the first and second years of college. The Lifetime Learning Credit is available for four years of study to eligible taxpayers. Visit www.nasfaa.org/Redesign/TaxBenefits guide.html for more details on these tax credits.

College Savings Programs include two types of 529 plans:

- Savings plans
- Pre-paid tuition plans.

Section 529 savings plans are tax advantaged accounts which can be used to pay tuition and other education-related expenses. These plans vary by state and you can invest in plans from other states. Upromise.com is a college savings program, which is a stress-free way to accumulate free money for college. Parents, students, and even grandparents or other relatives register their credit, gas, and shopping cards in a student's name. Purchases of gas, food, meals, and other items earn income in a student's account, which can be linked to a 529 savings plan. There are no strings attached, and there is no cost to the student. Go to www.upromise.com and register to start earning money for college.

Prepaid tuition plans, also known as *guaranteed savings plans*, give you an opportunity to prepay tuition in 13 states as well as at some educational institutions.

College credit programs include the Advanced Placement (AP) program, the College Level Examination Program (CLEP), the International Baccalaureate (IB) program, and college level courses offered in your high school. Through the AP and CLEP programs run by the College Board, you can receive credit for college courses by taking AP courses and examinations, if they are offered by your school. CLEP exams may be passed by taking college preparatory classes and studying for these exams. Visit www.collegeboard.com for more information on AP and CLEP exams. If your high school offers rigorous IB classes, you can take the IB exams to try to obtain college credit. Visit www.ibo.org for more information about IB courses and exams.

Some high schools offer college courses associated with a local college. You must obtain a certain grade in the course to receive credit, and you need to check with the colleges you are interested in attending to determine if the colleges accept the credits from these college courses. By receiving college credit through these programs, students may increase their chances of graduating in four years or earlier, thereby reducing college costs.

How do I apply for financial aid?

Many students and their parents dread filling out financial aid forms. You may have heard horror stories about how difficult it is to complete financial aid applications. The reality is that in most cases, you only need to complete one financial aid form to be considered for federal, state, and college-sponsored aid.

The form every student applying to college should complete is the Free Application for Federal Student Aid, known as FAFSA. To view the eligibility requirements, directions, worksheet, and online and paper applications, go to www.fafsa.ed.gov for the government's free Web site. If you inadvertently go to the similarly named private Web site (fafsa.com), you will be charged a fee for the same application, so be careful typing in the Web site address.

Some private colleges may also require you to complete the CSS/Financial Aid PROFILE, a fee-based service, which is part of College Board. In addition, some colleges may have their own financial aid application.

Filling Out the FAFSA

Some people believe the FAFSA is too long and complicated. There is a movement towards simplifying the FAFSA, so changes to the form may be in the works. For now though, filing a FAFSA consists of completing an online application, the preferred method of applying, as soon as possible after January 1st of your senior year. An online FAFSA is error proof as the online version helps you detect and correct errors as you are completing the application. It also uses "skip logic," which allows you to skip questions that don't pertain to you. A paper version can be used; it is available to download, but it does not have the same benefits as the online version.

Before completing the FAFSA, you can obtain an unofficial estimate of your eligibility for student aid by completing a FAFSA4Caster. It is recommended that you use the 4Caster to give you an accurate estimate of what you might receive in financial aid, so you can properly plan for college expenses. A FAFSA On the Web worksheet can also be downloaded to use as a guide when completing the online FAFSA. Completing the worksheet saves you time, as you will then be able to plug in the numbers line by line.

How do I get a PIN?

A Personal Identification Number (PIN) is also needed to complete the online FAFSA. This number can be obtained the November or December prior to the January 1st start date of the FAFSA. A PIN can be secured at www.pin.ed.gov by providing your name, date of birth, and correct Social Security number. You can generate your own secure code or one can be given to you. You should print or jot down your number, as the link to your PIN will only be available for a short time. The PIN serves as your legal electronic signature on the online FAFSA. Both you and one parent have to obtain PINs and sign if you are a dependent student. If you are an independent student, a parent does not need to sign the form. The FAFSA Web site explains how to determine whether you have dependent or independent status.

Once you are ready to file your FAFSA, you will need a valid Social Security number, a driver's license (optional), your tax returns and your parents' tax returns, W-2s, bank statements, and records of assets and investments for you and your parents. After you complete the FAFSA, you sign electronically with your PIN, or you can print out the paper application and mail it in within 14 days.

There are five sections to complete on the FAFSA:

- **Section 1: Student Information:** Complete your name, Social Security number, state of residence, drug convictions, questions about the educational status of your parents, information about attending college part time or full time, and whether you will consider work study and loans.

- **Section 2: Student Dependency Status:** Includes questions about military duty, veteran status, dependent or independent status.

- **Section 3: Parent Information:** Includes questions about parents' Social Security numbers, date of birth, tax information, and assets and investments.

- **Section 4: Student Finances:** Answer questions about student's assets and tax information.

- **Section 5: College Information:** List names of colleges and housing information. You can list up to 10 colleges on the online application and up to 4 colleges on the paper application.

For assistance completing the FAFSA, you can request live online help or you can call a customer service number. The process after completing the FAFSA is as follows:

Completed FAFSA ☞ US Department of Education Processing Center ☞ Expected Family Contribution (EFC) ☞ Student Aid Report (SAR)

A need analysis is completed by the colleges you are considering. This is done using the expected family contribution (EFC), determined by the completed FAFSA. The EFC is a critical number which is obtained by completing the FAFSA. The EFC is exactly what the name implies; it is the amount of money your family is expected to contribute annually to finance your education.

> You will receive your SAR (Student Aid Report) usually within three weeks of completing the FAFSA. If you include your e-mail on the FAFSA, you will receive the SAR by e-mail; if no e-mail is given, you will receive the SAR by mail.

Financial need is computed as follows:

Cost of Attendance – Expected Financial Contribution = Need

FAFSA FAQs

Here are some common questions about the FAFSA; the answers to these questions are provided by our financial aid experts:

Should I file a FAFSA even though my parents think they make too much money for financial aid?

"Absolutely! It's like the lottery, 'you have to be in it, to win it!' The form itself only takes a short time to complete and it is relatively straightforward. The worst thing that might happen is that students find out they are eligible for loans and no other aid. But in many cases, schools use the FAFSA to determine their own institutional aid awards. Private schools often award need-based monies to students even if the federal and state governments do not. Without the FAFSA, schools have nothing to base their decisions on. It's absolutely worth the effort!"–Jacquelyn Nealon, EdD, VP, Enrollment Services, New York Institute of Technology (NYIT)

"The FAFSA form is required by all colleges and helps determine eligibility for grants, loans, and work-study programs. While family income may help determine the types and amount of aid, it will not preclude a student from being considered for loans. Since there is no cost, other than a family's time, to complete the FAFSA, we would strongly encourage everyone interested in financial aid to complete it."–Dominic Yoia, Senior Director of Financial Aid, Quinnipiac University

When should I file a FAFSA? Do I need to wait for my parents to complete their taxes before filing a FAFSA or should I file as soon as possible after January 1st?

"In order to be considered for maximum availability of aid, students should complete the FAFSA as soon after January 1st as possible, and preferably prior to February 15th. Since most students need the financial aid package from the schools in order to make an informed decision about whether they can afford to attend, applying early gives families the time they need to weigh their offers and make a sound choice. It is better to do a good, close estimate and get the form in prior to February 15th than it is to wait if the taxes are going to be done much beyond then. The key is a close estimate. A difference of a few thousand dollars should not impact the package greatly. Keep in mind, some colleges have their own recommended deadlines that may differ from what I've just suggested. Students should definitely check with the financial aid offices of the colleges they are applying to just to be safe."–Jacquelyn Nealon, EdD, VP Enrollment Services, NYIT

"The FAFSA can be completed anytime after January 1st and families are advised to complete the form as early as possible using estimated data in order to meet institutional financial aid deadlines. Since a student's initial filing data never changes, updates can be made to the FAFSA once the federal tax returns have been completed in order to assure accuracy to both the FAFSA form as well as a student's financial aid award." –Dominic Yoia, Senior Director of Financial Aid, Quinnipiac University

WHAT IS THE CSS PROFILE AND HOW DO I KNOW IF I HAVE TO FILE ONE?

The CSS Profile is an additional financial aid form used by some colleges and universities to award non-federal aid. The Profile captures more detailed financial and demographic data about families.When you apply to colleges, the application instructions usually indicate if a CSS Profile is required for financial aid consideration. Since the form is administered by College Board (for a fee), you can check collegeboard.com for more information about participating colleges, universities, and scholarship programs.

What is in a financial aid package?

In March or April, sometimes earlier, you will receive a financial aid package from each college you indicated on the FAFSA. A financial aid letter will consist of scholarships, loans, grants, and work study. Some colleges will meet your full need and others will not meet your full need.

Let's take a look at the financial aid awards of three fictitious families to determine how families with varying needs are awarded financial aid. In the examples that follow, note how grants, scholarships, loans, and work study are combined to form a total financial aid package.

EXAMPLES OF FINANCIAL AID PACKAGES

Student A

Student A is applying to an in-state public university.

Cost of attendance (annual costs)	$15,000
EFC as determined by the FAFSA	$7,000
Need (COA – EFC)	$8,000

Financial aid package for Student A:

State grant	$1,000
Private scholarships	$2,000
Academic competitive grant	$750
Grant from public university	$2,000
Unsubsidized federal Stafford loan	$2,000
Unmet Need	$250

Analysis: Student A received $5,750 in grants and scholarships, which do not need to be paid back. Student A's parents will have to contribute $7,250 towards the COA, $7,000 of which is the EFC and $250 of which is unmet need. However, the rest of the financial aid package consists of $2,000 in loans, which will have to be paid by the student.

Student B

Student B is applying to a private university.

Cost of attendance (annual costs)	$45,000
EFC as determined by the FAFSA	$7,000
Need (COA – EFC)	$38,000

Financial aid package for Student B:

Federal Pell Grant	$4,000
Federal work study	$2,500
State grants	$3,000
Private university grant	$15,000
Private scholarships	$10,000
Subsidized Stafford loan	$3,500
Unmet Need	$0

Analysis: Student B received $32,000 in grants and scholarships which do not need to be paid back. Student B will be offered a part-time job on campus, from which the student will earn $2,500. Student B will be expected to pay back $3,500 in low-interest loans. Student B's parents are expected to pay $7,000 towards the COA.

Student C

Student C is applying to an out-of-state public university.

Cost of attendance (annual costs)	$30,000
EFC as determined by the FAFSA	$22,000
Need (COA – EFC)	$8,000

Financial aid package for Student C:

State grant	$1,000
Public university grant	$3,000
Private scholarships	$2,000
Unsubsidized Stafford loan	$2,000
Unmet Need	$0

Analysis: Student C received $6,000 in grants and scholarships, which do not need to be paid back. Student C can accept an unsubsidized federal Stafford loan of $2,000 which will need to be paid back by the student. Student C's parents are expected to pay $22,000 towards the COA.

When comparing award letters from colleges, you need to find out:

- Is there a minimum GPA you need to maintain in order to receive any grants or scholarships?

- How much of the award consists of scholarships/grants that do not have to be paid back, and how much of the award consists of loans that do have to be paid back?

- If work study is included, how much will you be paid, what jobs are available, and how many hours will you be working?

- Is the award being given for only one year, or is the award renewable for up to four years?

CAN YOU APPEAL YOUR FINANCIAL AID PACKAGE?

What do you do if you don't get the financial aid package you need in order to attend the college of your choice?

If you have received a financial aid package and you are not satisfied with the amount you received, you can appeal. Dominic Yoia, Senior Director of Financial Aid at Quinnipiac University, says, "It never hurts to ask. If a college has not met all of a student's need, has additional funds available, or for some reason feels that additional aid is warranted, they may enhance the initial award to help the student in paying their educational expenses. While I am not advocating every student 'cry wolf,' there are instances, especially if a student or family is experiencing financial difficulties, where sitting down with the appropriate college representative is appropriate."

Financial aid officers may re-evaluate a financial aid package if there has been a change in a financial situation. According to Jacquelyn Nealon, VP for Enrollment Services at NYIT, in cases where modest amounts of funds are needed for students to attend a dream school, "there is no harm in making a phone call to that one school to ask for a small amount of additional funding. The student just needs to be prepared in the event that no new monies are available . . . what's the backup plan?"

The chart on the next page may assist you in comparing aid from different colleges. To complete the chart, you need to know the COA, which includes tuition, fees, room, board, and transportation, and the EFC, which is in the SAR you received after completing the FAFSA.

COMPARING AID PACKAGES WORKSHEET

ITEM	COLLEGE 1	COLLEGE 2	COLLEGE 3
Cost of Attendance	$	$	$
	SUBTRACT	SUBTRACT	SUBTRACT
Expected Family Contribution (EFC)	$	$	$
= Need Award Package	$	$	$
Grants	$	$	$
Loans	$	$	$
Scholarships	$	$	$
Work Study	$	$	$
Total Financial Aid	$	$	$
	SUBTRACT	SUBTRACT	SUBTRACT
Need	$	$	$
= Unmet Need	$	$	$

How can I apply for scholarships?

Scholarships are an excellent source of money to help pay for college. Some scholarships are need based, some are merit (academic) based, and others are a combination of the two. There are different types of scholarships; here is a list of places to consult for various types:

- **Athletic scholarships:** Information is available at www.ncaa.org.
- **Corporate scholarships:** The National Merit Scholarship Corporation (NMSC) offers merit scholarships based on PSAT scores, and QuestBridge Scholarships are based on merit and financial need. Many major organizations offer scholarships; sample scholarships are listed in the appendices.
- **Community/Civic/Local organizations:** Some local organizations, including the Kiwanis Club, Knights of Columbus, Knights of Pythias, Lions Club, and others, offer scholarships.
- **Colleges:** Many colleges offer scholarships based on the major being studied, "first-generation" (first student in a family to attend college) scholarships, and others. Check the college's Web site or call the financial aid office for more information.
- **Your high school:** Many guidance counselors know about local, state, and national awards as well as scholarship money given to students at graduation.
- **Unions and professional/trade organizations:** Many unions, including teachers' unions, offer scholarships to their families, and professional organizations also offer scholarships. Check with your parents' employers for potential scholarships.

Searching for scholarships can be time consuming and frustrating. Money is available from different sources, but you may have to do a lot of legwork and fill out a lot of applications. You can use free scholarship searches to find potential scholarships, including:

- www.fastweb.com
- www.finaid.org
- www.meritaid.com
- Other scholarship Web sites are listed in Appendix B

Depending on the scholarship you apply for, you may be required to submit transcripts, essays, letters of recommendations, and SAT/ACT scores. To maximize your chances of receiving a scholarship, be sure to:

- Follow directions (only apply if you meet the eligibility requirements).
- Enclose all required documents.
- File the scholarship on time.
- Focus more on applying to local scholarships, as competition for national scholarships is fierce.

- Concentrate on putting together several smaller scholarships rather than trying for larger scholarships, which may be out of reach for you.

- Write a terrific scholarship essay.

- Ace your scholarship interview, if one is required.

- Have others advocate on your behalf and ask friends and relatives to notify you of any scholarships they come across.

How can I avoid scholarship scams?

Unfortunately, there are many unscrupulous people out there who take advantage of students and their parents in the search for scholarship money.

My daughter, a high school junior, has received many letters that sound and look promising. These letters can be misleading, and they give false hope to people anxious to get money for college. Some letters you receive have expensive packaging. They imply you have already been scheduled to participate in a group presentation and interview, or they imply your high school authorized them to contact you. You can check on scholarship or financial aid companies by contacting the following organizations:

> There are so many free resources and Web sites available that it really is unnecessary to hire a scholarship or financial aid consultant.

- Better Business Bureau (www.bbb.com)

- Postal Inspectors (postalinspectors.uspis.gov)

- Attorney Generals (www.naag.org)

You may wonder if it is advisable to hire a financial consultant to help you figure out how to pay for college. Jacquelyn Nealon, VP Enrollment Services, NYIT, does not recommend it: "There is really nothing that complex about the financial aid application process that families cannot accomplish on their own. With a copy of a tax return at the ready, you have all the answers you need to complete the forms. And the colleges are very willing and able to explain the financial aid award letters and how to determine actual costs to attend. In these tough times, I'd rather see families put the money they would spend on these consultants toward the student's tuition."

Dominic Yoia, Senior Director of Financial Aid at Quinnipiac University, concurs: "Like most businesses, there are some that are reputable and others with questionable intentions. Unfortunately, my experience has found the majority of these 'consultants' to be less than honorable, oftentimes charging thousands of dollars while not providing much more information than a family could have found with minimal effort on their own. In extreme cases, these folks have been known to coerce families into providing false or misleading information; translation—financial aid fraud. The best advice I can offer to families seeking paid consultation is the old adage, 'if it looks too good to be true, it usually is.' Should a family need financial aid advice, the best place to start is with its college's financial aid office. There are also many reputable, certified CPAs [certified public accountants] who are happy to help their clients, usually for a nominal fee, in completing the FAFSA form while they also prepare the family tax returns."

What are some tips and techniques for financial aid?

Our financial aid officers suggest the following tips when applying for financial aid:

What financial aid advice do you have for students in times of economic distress?

"While the FAFSA form gathers basic financial and demographic information, it is not a comprehensive enough form to assess a family's complete financial picture. Families experiencing financial hardships are encouraged to contact their college's financial aid office to discuss the merits of their situation, and oftentimes, a counselor may be able to suggest additional financing options or re-evaluate the aid being offered."–Dominic Yoia, Senior. Director of Financial Aid, Quinnipiac University

"Do your heavy lifting up front. There are 4,000 colleges and universities in this country… one at every price point. Researching schools in terms of affordability is as important as researching them in terms of academic and social fit. By selecting colleges that are within financial reach, you can ensure that no matter what, you'll be able to attend college. If your family has experienced an unusual financial circumstance within the last year, you'll want to put together a documentation packet that explains what has changed, what impact it has had on the family's financial situation, and what the projected income for the coming year is likely to be. Then each institution will conduct a professional judgment review to determine if a change is warranted in the financial aid package."–Jacquelyn Nealon, VP Enrollment Services, NYIT

What advice do you have for an average student whose parents are middle- to upper-middle class?

"They should feel no different than any other student! The expectation, of course, is the more financial ability a family has, the less need-based aid they require; however, there are lots of different financial aid programs available to assist students from all types of backgrounds. While some financial aid is targeted to students who demonstrate financial need, other types recognize students with strong academic qualifications, special talents, athletic ability, community service, or a variety of other credentials."–Dominic Yoia, Senior Director of Financial Aid, Quinnipiac University

"There is a school for everyone! Every student who wishes to attend college this fall can go. The key is to keep your eyes on the prize: a college degree. What matters most is that a student attends college…that is even more important than 'which' college a student attends. Diversify the schools you apply to in order to ensure that you have at least a few affordable options. For some folks, that may be a two-year public or a low-priced private. It's going to be different for every family."–Jacquelyn Nealon, VP Enrollment Services, NYIT

Do you have any other advice regarding financial aid?

"The best advice I can offer students is to be diligent, be resourceful, and take ownership in their education by applying for everything they can find. Quite often, when we see students getting outside scholarships, they get more than one because they've applied for many. There are also lots of other financial opportunities on a college campus, including work-study programs, paid internships, community service, or student leadership positions that may come with stipends such as serving as a resident assistant or in student government. So, the three key words are *apply, apply, apply!*"–Dominic Yoia, Senior Director of Financial Aid, Quinnipiac University

What if the economy is bad?

Financial aid becomes even more critical when there are periods of economic crisis. Some families respond by coaching their teens to choose financially affordable schools. Other families allow their children to go ahead and enroll in their first-choice college, even though the cost of attendance is very high. Each family ultimately has to do what's comfortable for them. Wealthier families may have an advantage in the admissions process during uncertain economic times, because colleges prefer full-pay students. Full-pay students are students who indicate on the college application that they are not applying for financial aid and can pay the full sticker price for a college.

Many colleges are committed to encouraging low-income and minority students to apply, so some colleges try to increase the financial aid offered to these students. The financial aid process is a tricky one, and policies can change from year to year. Some colleges which were previously need blind may change their policy. It is critical that students and their parents have open and honest communications with each other and with financial aid officers during the college admissions process.

Avoiding Roadblocks and Hazards

"I should have studied more for the SAT/ACT exams."

"I can't believe I missed a financial aid deadline."

"I wish my parents weren't so involved in the application process."

The college admissions process is a multifaceted and complex one, with many details and deadlines. To avoid hitting roadblocks and potential hazards along the way, the best way to prepare is to be proactive, plan ahead, and do extensive research. Being *proactive* means starting early and anticipating potential problems, so that you can deal with them before they strike.

If you truly want to be prepared, you can start preparing for college as early as ninth grade by following the steps discussed in Chapter 2:

- 🎓 Take challenging courses
- 🎓 Involve yourself in a few activities in an area of passion or interest
- 🎓 Attain consistent grades or have grades on an upward trend

If you wait until senior year to wake up and begin the process, you can still catch up and get admitted to a college which suits your needs, but you will be way ahead of the game if you start early. Chapter 9 reveals what strategies you can follow if you're getting a late start.

How can I be proactive?

You can be proactive in the college search process by:

- 🎓 Conducting an honest self-assessment (covered in Chapter 1)
- 🎓 Being realistic about your finances and your chances of being admitted

- Doing research, research, and more research (discussed in chapters 3 and 4)
- Engaging in extracurricular activities beginning in ninth grade
- Demonstrating interest in colleges and making your application stand out (reviewed in Chapter 6)
- Being aware of deadlines and requirements (use the calendars and checklists in chapters 1 and 6)
- Taking personal responsibility for your academic history, and following up during the application process (covered in chapters 6 and 10)

SELF ASSESSMENT

Back in Chapter 1, we covered the importance of doing a self-assessment. Before embarking on a college search, you must take a step back and really think about who you are and where you're going. You should assess your personality, your values, your needs, and your wants. If you can do this honestly, it will be easier to make a choice later on, as you will be able to determine if a college fits your needs, realizing that there is a "multi-fit" approach to choosing colleges.

REALISTIC CHOICES

Be realistic during your college quest, in terms of your chances of being admitted and the economic reality of your situation. Chapter 3 discussed what students should look for when evaluating colleges and Chapter 7 reviewed the economic aspects of college.

Do's and don'ts for picking realistic college choices

- Don't waste time applying to colleges truly out of your reach.
- Listen to your counselor.
- Look at the "Common Data Set" or Freshman Profile to see if you are in the range to be considered for admission.
- Have a conversation with your family in the early stages of your search to discuss how much your family can realistically afford.
- Have your parents use the FAFSA4caster to project college expenses.
- Don't set yourself up for disappointment by applying to colleges out of reach for you academically or financially.

RESEARCH YOUR CHOICES WISELY

Conducting research during the application process increases your chances of finding an appropriate college where you will thrive academically and socially. Chapter 3 reviewed the

> **TIP:** Think "outside the box" when choosing colleges. Consider colleges in different geographical locations. You might be pleasantly surprised with these choices, so have an open mind in the initial research phase.

factors to consider in choosing a college, and Chapter 4 presented information about what to look for when visiting campuses.

Here are some suggestions when researching colleges:

🎓 Apply to a manageable number of schools in different ranges (highly likely/ probable, likely/target, and not likely/ reach schools—these terms are defined in Chapter 3).

🎓 Each school on your list should be one where you can see yourself being happy academically and socially. Don't apply to name-brand colleges just because other students are applying there; choose schools that are right for you.

🎓 Become familiar with a college's requirements for admission as well as what it offers and what requirements (including general education or core requirements) are needed to graduate.

> *"Research, research, research. This process can seem mind-boggling at times, but the more you know, the more you're in a position to end up making a good decision. Students should keep an active list handy of questions they want to ask about every college they consider. That list should be ever-evolving with additions and deletions as they go through the process. They should contact every college they're considering and read their materials (both printed and online). Even 'local' resources like (dare I say it?) parents, other relatives, neighbors, etc. can be helpful."*
>
> –Lorne Robinson, Dean of Admissions and Financial Aid, Macalester College

START EXTRACURRICULAR ACTIVITIES EARLY

If you truly want to be proactive, you should start participating in extracurricular activities in ninth grade. Don't participate in activities because they look good on your resume; engage in activities which you truly enjoy and which reflect your potential interests. The best way to explore potential interests is by being involved from day one when you enter high school. Colleges look for consistency and increasing responsibility, so try to grow with an activity and take on increasing leadership in that activity. Refer back to the planning calendar in Chapter 1 to ensure you attend club fairs to find activities of interest to you.

ACTIONS SPEAK LOUDER THAN WORDS: HOW TO STAND OUT

It is important for you to distinguish yourself from other applicants and to demonstrate your interest in colleges. Chapter 4 provided you with tips and strategies for visiting colleges and Chapter 6 advised you how to make your applications stand out.

Ways to demonstrate your interest in a college include:

🎓 **Requesting information.** You (not your parents) should contact colleges and request information. Do your homework and ask thoughtful questions. Mitchell Thompson, Dean of Students at Scarsdale High School, says, "Take part in tours and participate in overnights if and where possible. Additionally, communicating with an admissions officer after meeting at a college fair, during a high school visit, or while on a college campus is important. A good number of schools note when students have demonstrated genuine interest; just know one's boundaries. And once again it is important to ask relevant questions and be sincere in all communications."

- ☛ **Requesting an interview.** An interview, if offered, gives you a way to communicate your interest directly to an admissions officer, alumnus, or student.

- ☛ **Attending an information session and campus tour.** Cheryl Brown, Director of Undergraduate Admissions at Binghamton University, says, "Visiting the campus is the best way to know if a school is the right fit."

- ☛ **Meeting admissions representatives at your high school.** This idea, discussed in Chapter 3, is another way to communicate your interest and meet people who are making admissions decisions.

- ☛ **Maintaining contact with admissions officers.** Through e-mail you can update admissions officers with new information about your application, including grades and extracurricular activities.

- ☛ **Joining Facebook groups and blogs.** Technology is of growing importance in the admissions process. As discussed in Chapter 2, however, be careful what you post on various Web sites. Do not post any information that could be potentially embarrassing, and keep in mind that parents, admissions officers, and potential employers check these sites for inappropriate material. It is strongly suggested that before you submit any applications, you review your online postings to ensure nothing could jeopardize your admission.

- ☛ **Visiting colleges before you apply.** Use what you know about the college in writing your essays in order to demonstrate specifically why a college is a good fit for you.

It is vital that you demonstrate your interest in various ways, as some colleges track their communications with students throughout the entire process to gauge their interest. Raymond Lutzky, Director of Outreach at Rensselaer Polytechnic Institute, says, "Rensselaer tracks every single touch-point with a student, from attendance at an on-campus event to meeting a volunteer at a college fair on the other side of the country. When the admissions committee reviews an application, they see a record of every opportunity the student took to connect with the university."

According to our panel of admissions counselors, the best way to convince other college admissions counselors to accept you is by making your applications stand out.

- ☛ Mitchell Thompson from Scarsdale High School advises that you advocate for yourself, take risks, and be yourself. Write convincing and sincere essays that reflect your values and personality. Chapter 5 reviews ways to make your essay stand out.

- Cheryl Brown from Binghamton University suggests that you think about how you can best present yourself, which includes writing a strong essay, serving in leadership roles, and explaining why you're a great fit for a particular university.

- Lauren Kay from Indiana University and Nancy Maly from Grinnell College suggest that you focus on taking challenging courses and doing well in those courses (covered in Chapter 2). You also need to choose wisely which teachers to ask for letters of recommendation (also mentioned in Chapter 2).

- Raymond Lutzky from Rensselaer Polytechnic Institute recommends you show your excitement about attending a particular college by getting "in the face of your first-choice college without appearing annoying or immature." He also recommends that you visit a college more than once and mention any family connections or other information which highlights your interest in a college.

KEEP TRACK OF DEADLINES AND REQUIREMENTS

You can hit a major roadblock in college admissions if you don't pay attention to deadlines for registering for tests and for applying to colleges. Use the planning calendar in Chapter 1 to record important deadlines. As discussed in Chapter 6, there are many pieces of the application which you need to compile and then track to ensure your application is in on time. You need to send all of your test scores, give teachers sufficient notice to write letters, and start your essays way before they are due.

> *"Take the crisis out of the process of applying to college and you'll be far more relaxed when you're waiting for decisions."*
>
> —Joan Mohr, VP and Dean of Admissions at Quinnipiac University

TAKE PERSONAL RESPONSIBILITY

You are responsible for your own behavior in college. Due to privacy laws, colleges are not permitted to talk to your parents, so you need to learn to advocate for yourself. Your responsibilities include

- Verifying that your transcript is accurate.

- Checking that your application is complete and that all of your documents and scores have been received by colleges.

- Not blaming others for poor grades, missed opportunities, or not knowing what to do during the process.

- Staying informed—read your high school Guidance Department's Web site, newsletters, and handbooks.

- Asking questions! Don't be in the dark and say, "No one told me."

How can I avoid mistakes?

Mistakes during the college admissions process can cost you money as well as your acceptance to the college of your choice. Of course, the best way to avoid mistakes is to plan ahead, keep track of deadlines, and have an ongoing dialogue with your parents and your counselor.

Let's take a look at 10 of the most common mistakes made during the college admissions process, and review ways to avoid them and actions to take if a mistake occurs.

> **TIP:** If you are taking a test on standby, get to the test center very early, so you are one of the first standby test takers, ensuring you will be able to take the exam.

MISTAKE #1: MISSING THE SAT/ACT REGISTRATION DEADLINE

Avoidance Strategy: Place the SAT/ACT registration deadlines on a planning calendar (Chapter 1).

Corrective Strategies: Some students put off taking standardized tests until senior year. The good news is that you can still take the SAT/ACT for the first time even in the fall or spring of your senior year, especially if you apply to colleges with later deadlines. If you are a junior and you missed the regular registration deadline and the late registration deadline, you can try taking a test on "standby," where you show up the day of the test. Test centers usually have a few extra copies of the exam, because some students decide at the last minute not to take the test.

MISTAKE #2: NOT PREPARING ADEQUATELY FOR THE SAT/ACT

Avoidance Strategy: Register for an online course and prepare as much as you can before the test. There are also test preparation books geared toward studying for the SAT/ACT.

Corrective Strategy: Register for another test and learn from your mistake by preparing in advance.

MISTAKE #3: MAKING MISTAKES ON YOUR APPLICATION OR ESSAY

Avoidance Strategy: Carefully proofread your application and essay for grammatical or other errors. Have another person (a teacher, parent, or counselor) check over your essays.

Corrective Strategy: If you realize a mistake was made on your essay or application, send a corrected paper copy and instruct the admissions office to replace your essay or information that you already submitted with your corrected essay or information. You can also call the Admissions Office for specific instructions.

> *"When you are writing what I call the "Why College X" essay—that is, the essay that often supplements the personal statement—make sure that you put the right college name in it. Sometimes applicants adapt one essay for several colleges, but fail to check to make sure they have inserted the right college name in every case."*
>
> —Paul Marthers, Dean of Admission, Reed College

MISTAKE #4: NOT ADEQUATELY RESEARCHING COLLEGES

Avoidance Strategy: Review your list of colleges and determine if you would be happy attending every college on your list.

Corrective Strategy: Check to see which colleges are still accepting applications, and apply to a few more schools after you've done some research and visited.

MISTAKE #5: MISSING AN APPLICATION DEADLINE

Avoidance Strategy: Show your respect for the process by submitting all required materials by the deadline indicated on the application.

Corrective Strategy: Call the Admissions Office and ask if they will accept a late application, and apply to a few more colleges.

MISTAKE #6: NOT FILING THE FAFSA AND OTHER FINANCIAL AID FORMS ON TIME

Avoidance Strategy: *Do not miss these deadlines*—the sooner you file, the better. Use the planning calendar in Chapter 1 to track FAFSA and other deadlines.

> *"A 'mistake' to avoid is to demonstrate a lack of respect for our process. If we ask you to submit certain materials by a deadline and you miss the deadline, that's a mistake."*
>
> —Jacquelyn Nealon, VP, Enrollment Services, NYIT

Corrective Strategy: File the financial aid documents ASAP, and call the Financial Aid Office for advice.

MISTAKE #7: OVERLY INVOLVING YOUR PARENTS IN THE COLLEGE PROCESS

Avoidance Strategy: Talk to your parents in the beginning of the process and tell them you want their advice but that you will take the lead on things and they shouldn't become overly involved.

Corrective Strategy: If you realize your parents are becoming overly involved, ask them gently to back off and demonstrate to them that you are taking responsibility for the process.

> "If you call the admissions office (or worse, have your parents call the admissions office) too frequently to check on the status of your application, it can become a distraction."–Jacquelyn Nealon, VP, Enrollment Services, NYIT
>
> "Applicants (and especially their parents) should not badger colleges by phone or e-mail. You never want to be the applicant whose name is well known to the admissions office due to repeated phone calls and e-mails."–Paul Marthers, Dean of Admission, Reed College

MISTAKE #8: NOT VISITING COLLEGES BEFORE YOU APPLY

Avoidance Strategy: Try to visit most colleges before you apply, unless they are very far away. You will then be able to adequately answer the "Why are you applying?" essay.

Corrective Strategy: Take a day off from school and visit your top choices. If you have to, visit colleges after you are accepted but before the "universal reply date" of May 1, unless you are applying to colleges with later deadlines.

MISTAKE #9: FORGETTING TO SEND YOUR SAT/ACT SCORES TO COLLEGES

Avoidance Strategy: An application is not considered complete until all of your documents are received, including your official SAT and ACT scores. You can avoid this scenario by listing your colleges when you register for a test, listing your colleges on your admissions ticket and bringing it in the day of the test, or going online and sending your scores within a few days of the test. If you want to see your scores first before you send them in, you can send scores (usually for a fee) after you receive them.

Corrective Strategy: If you check your online status or you receive a letter or e-mail indicating that your file is incomplete because you are missing test scores, you can go online to your College Board and/or ACT accounts and send your scores to colleges. You will have to pay a fee to send your scores to each college. You do not usually need to "rush" your scores for an additional fee, but check with each college. Colleges will still accept documents after the deadline, and your application will be reviewed when it is complete.

MISTAKE #10: MISSING SCHOLARSHIP DEADLINES

Avoidance Strategy: Obtaining free money for college is too important, so *don't miss scholarship deadlines*. Start your scholarship search early, in your sophomore or junior year. You can keep a scholarship file and obtain all of the necessary documents in order to meet scholarship deadlines.

Corrective Strategy: If you miss a scholarship deadline, call and ask if you can send the application a few days late. Otherwise, look for other scholarships with later deadlines.

Getting a Late Start

> *It's never too late to apply as there are many colleges that are rolling admissions schools, meaning they continue to accept applications throughout the year. Salvaging a senior year is tricky . . . but worth doing if you're serious about getting into college. Work with teachers to do extra-credit assignments, show a grade trend that is on the rise, and get letters of recommendation from teachers and guidance counselors who speak to your improved work ethic and school work.*
>
> –Jacquelyn Nealon, VP of Enrollment Services, New York Institute of Technology

If you're like many teenagers, you procrastinate even with something as important as applying to college. Some students wait until senior year because they are in denial or they are afraid of leaving their friends and family. They figure if they delay applying to college, it lessens the fear of leaving high school. Other students are simply lazy or too laid back. Unfortunately, colleges are not knocking down your door waiting for you to apply, so you really need to respect their deadlines.

If you've waited until senior year to get your act together, it is not too late to apply and pull together a cohesive and strong application, but don't delay too long. Colleges that are seeing substantial increases in applications or cuts in enrollment could stop accepting applications earlier than their posted application deadlines, so get moving!

Where do I start?

If you've waited until senior year to research colleges, you have a lot to do in order to meet remaining application deadlines. If you haven't taken the SAT/ACT exams yet, you can still register, prepare for, and take these exams through January, even March, of your senior year. Check the SAT/ACT deadlines and register online at www.collegeboard.com or www.act.org.

To get ready for these exams, sign up for an online course where you can work at your own pace, find a test preparation class that's starting soon, or obtain a tutor.

You also need to work on essays and prepare an extracurricular activities list or résumé. You should ask two academic teachers who you feel can write strong letters of recommendation. You might want to consider asking at least one teacher, who can indicate you are focused on doing well in your senior year. If you are a student who is a late bloomer, ask the teacher writing a letter to focus on the positive trend in your grades. Colleges appreciate honesty, so if your grades were not so hot in freshman or sophomore year but your grades dramatically improved the last two years, you should emphasize this in your essay.

If you have not been too involved in extracurricular activities, don't load up on activities in senior year, as colleges are not easily fooled by this strategy. Rather, try to involve yourself in one or two activities which are closely related to an interest you're especially passionate about, and indicate you will continue these interests in college. If you have an extenuating circumstance and you are unable to participate in extracurricular activities, this should be mentioned on the application.

If you haven't visited a single college, again it is not too late. Although it is preferable to visit schools before you apply, you can still visit colleges in February, March, and April, before the May 1 reply deadline. If you are applying to colleges with later deadlines than May 1, you can continue your college visits through the spring and summer. Focus on choosing and applying to a few highly likely, target, and financially affordable colleges to increase your chances of being admitted, especially if you have an inconsistent transcript. Research colleges online and narrow down your choices to a few colleges which you know you would be happy to attend if accepted. Now is not the time to apply to a large list of unrealistic colleges. Apply only to those colleges which are realistic for you. You can also consider applying to a community college to prove that you are capable of successfully completing college courses. Credits usually transfer to four-year colleges, and tuition is typically cheaper.

Ignore those students who are in a senior slump, otherwise known as "senioritis." Your grades in your last year of high school are critical, and you need to demonstrate you have the academic ability to succeed in college. A "to-do" list is included at the end of this chapter to assist you in taking care of the many details that you need to accomplish in a short period of time.

What if I've missed some deadlines?

Fortunately, there are many colleges which have deadlines of February 1 or later, some as late as the summer. Of course, your chances of being admitted increase the earlier you apply, especially to colleges with rolling admission deadlines. However, there are plenty of colleges at different ends of the selectivity spectrum which offer later application deadlines. If you enter senior year without any college plans, you can still catch up and be ready to enter college in the fall. Just allow yourself the time and energy to focus on completing your applications, as it is a very time-consuming process. As mentioned in Chapter 3, using the Common App or Universal College Application may save you some valuable time.

> **NOTE:** It is not uncommon for application procrastinators to get a rejection letter, since it may appear they did not put enough thought or effort into the essays and other parts of the application.

Your guidance counselor is a valuable source of information about colleges with later deadlines. You also can check the Common Application and Universal College Application Web sites, as well as individual college Web sites for deadline information. Call colleges with deadlines that have passed to see if they will still accept your application if you get it in as soon as possible. Colleges that are under-enrolled for the fall may still accept your application. The following table shows some colleges that have deadlines of February 1 or later, so do your research and get started!

Colleges with Later Deadlines	
Adelphi University	March 1
Albright College	March 1
California State: Bakersfield, Fresno, Sacramento, San Bernadino	March 1
Canisius College	April 1
College of Santa Fe	August 31
Colorado State	July 1
Curry College	April 1
Drew University	February 15
Drexel University	March 1
Eckerd College	June 30
Franklin and Marshall College	February 1
Gustavus Adolphus College	May 10
Hartwick College	February 15
Hobart and William Smith College	February 1
Hofstra University	June 11
Iona College	February 15
Ithaca College	February 1
La Salle University	April 1
Le Moyne College	February 1
Manhattanville College	March 1
Marist College	February 15
Millsaps College	June 11
Muhlenberg College	February 15
Pace University	March 1
Quinnipiac University	February 1

continued

Richard Stockton College	May 1
Rochester Institute of Technology	February 1
Roger Williams University	February 1
Russell Sage College	June 11
Siena College	March 1
State University of New York—Albany	March 1
State University of New York—Cortland	May 31
State University of New York—Fredonia	May 1
State University of New York—New Paltz	April 1
State University of New York—Oneonta	April 1
Steven's Institute of Technology	February 1
University of Dallas	March 1
University of Iowa	April 1
University of Mary Washington	February 1
University of Massachusetts–Boston	June 1
University of New Haven	August 20
University of Portland	February 1
University of Scranton	March 1
University of Tulsa	March 1
Wabash College	February 1
Washington & Jefferson College	March 1
Xavier University	February 1

How can I salvage my senior year?

Senior year is an important year. Colleges expect you to take a full and challenging course load, and senior grades may still be requested by many colleges, especially highly selective ones. If you are a borderline student, senior year can be especially important to convince colleges you are serious academically. Colleges also know maturity is a factor for some students, so senior year is a time to prove yourself. If you are a student who had a slow start or inconsistent grades, your senior year may be a way for you to demonstrate your readiness for college.

As we discussed in Chapter 2, colleges look for a positive trend (grades that go up each year) and strong senior grades. Lorne Robinson, Dean of Admissions and Financial Aid at Macalester College, believes that "a student who's a 'late bloomer' is clearly going to be viewed more positively than one whose grades are declining in later years."

Deferring your college entrance for a year is another way to tackle a late start. Joan Mohr, VP and Dean of Admissions at Quinnipiac University, says, "not all students choose a 'traditional' path. Some will work or travel for the year after high school. Some will begin at a community college to strengthen their academic skills at a reasonable cost and take credits that will transfer on to a 4 year school, where they'll eventually receive their degree. It's never too late to get motivated."

Senior year "catch up" to-do list

If you have left most of the researching, planning, visiting, and applying until your senior year, you need to catch up on all of the steps needed to prepare an effective application. The following "to-do" list covers what you need to do if you are getting a late start.

> *"Preparation matters. Relying on last-minute inspirations is a kind of magical thinking akin to rolling the dice and expecting to get double sixes. Not having a strong academic or extracurricular record by the end of the junior year does put most applicants at a disadvantage. But getting on an upward trend will always help; no matter when it happens—even if it occurs as late as the senior year. Late bloomers may need to improve their records in a post-graduate high school year, or consider transferring after a year or two of strong grades at one of the colleges that will admit them, or try a gap year with some academic content to it."*
>
> –Paul Marthers, Dean of Admission at Reed College

Catch Up To-Do List		
Activity	✓	*Notes*
RESEARCH		
Review your transcript for accuracy		
Talk to parents and your guidance counselor		
Do a self assessment (Chapter 1)		
Select a few colleges you're sure you would attend, if accepted		
Visit colleges		

continued

Activity	✓	Notes
TESTING		
Set up a College Board/ACT account		
Register for exams and send scores to colleges		
Take SAT/ACT exams in the fall and spring of your senior year, as needed		
APPLICATIONS		
Ask two teachers for letters of recommendation		
Develop an extracurricular activities list/résumé		
Write a draft of your personal statement/essays		
Proofread your essay and ask two to three people for feedback		
Apply online, using Common App, Universal College Application, or the college's application		
Proofread applications before submitting		
Ensure all applications and documents are submitted		

Activity	✓	Notes
FOLLOW-UP		
Check your status online or call colleges		
Verify all documents have been submitted (two to three weeks after submitting)		
Review and evaluate offers of admission		
Notify the one college you are accepting and send a deposit		
Decline other offers of admission		

Where Do I Go from Here?

> *Congratulations! We are pleased to offer you admission to the Class of _____.*

These are the words you've been anxious to hear after you've been through the rigorous college applications process. You've completed your application, ensuring all of your documents have been received and checking that your file is complete. You've visited colleges and you've completed the FAFSA and other required financial aid forms. You're maintaining your GPA in your senior year, and now the moment of truth has arrived—getting replies from your colleges.

When will I be notified by colleges?

You will be notified by colleges at different times in your senior year, depending on how and when you applied. The chart below lists approximate dates for receiving decisions:

Type of Admission	Expected Date of Notification
Rolling	2–8 weeks from the date your application is complete
Early Decision	Mid–late December
Early Action	January–February
Early Decision II	February
Regular Decision (deadlines through Feb. 15)	March–April
Regular Decision (deadlines after Mar. 1)	April–late summer

How will I be notified?

There are several ways in which colleges inform you of their admission decision. There are no standardized methods for this important notification, so you can check with each college or your guidance counselor to find out how you will be notified. Possible options include:

- **Mail:** Some colleges still use good, old-fashioned snail mail.
- **Phone:** Some private colleges use the telephone to deliver good news.
- **E-mail:** You may receive an e-mail with your decision or you may be instructed to check your online account.
- **College Web site's online account:** If you have set up an account and have been given a user name and password, you may be able to "check your status" on the college's Web site in the admissions section. You should make sure to set up your account before decision notifications have begun to prevent any potential problems with logging in to your account.

Softening the Blow or Magnifying the Joy

Some online decisions are posted during the day, while students are still in school, which can be disruptive as well as upsetting to students who receive bad news. Because of this, many colleges post their decisions after 5:00 pm, when most students are home from school. Rejection letters are also getting a second look, as online rejections can at times be blunt and harsh. Some colleges are softening the language of rejection letters to alleviate some of the pain students may feel.

Alternatively, acceptances sent through the mail have become more ornate, with the goal of enticing students to accept a college's offer. As many students are applying to more schools, colleges want to encourage you to attend their college by sending you "perks," including T-shirts, posters, decals, and other college-specific souvenirs. Other colleges add a personal touch with links to celebratory videos, text messages, phone calls, and personalized letters.

What are the possible admissions decisions?

As we have discussed previously, applying early through rolling, early action, or early decision plans results in earlier notifications of college decisions. Notifications can consist of the following decisions:

- Rejection
- Deferred admission

- Conditional acceptance
- Acceptance
- Waitlist

REJECTION

An outright rejection is a possible outcome from schools which were your "reach" schools or from schools where your credentials were below what the college was looking for. Once the decision is made and after your initial heartbreak, it is best to focus on hearing from other potential schools. There may be some schools which offer an appeals process, where you can ask for a re-evaluation of your application based on new or additional information. You can ask the admissions office if this is a possible course of action for you.

DEFERRED ADMISSION

Being deferred from an early action or early decision school is a common notification which many schools use to "hedge their bets." They are not ruling out that you will be admitted, but they are waiting to see what type of students will apply during the regular decision process. If you are deferred, you can take that as a good sign your application is being considered, but it is not a guarantee you will eventually be admitted. You may want to keep in contact with your college admissions officer during this period to keep him or her updated on your recent activities and your continued interest in their college. If you are deferred, you will most likely receive your final college decision with the regular decision applicants.

CONDITIONAL ACCEPTANCE

A conditional acceptance is a possible notification if your application looks promising, but you may have a deficit in one or more areas, such as grades or SAT/ACT scores. A conditional acceptance may require you to take a reduced course load (taking fewer courses than other students) or to be placed on probation for the first semester or for the first year. Probation means your academic progress may be monitored to ensure you are not at risk of failing courses or dropping out of college. Another possible option is that you may be admitted to an alternate semester, such as summer or spring, or to an alternate campus. You should read your acceptance letters carefully to find out if you have been accepted to a university's main campus or to a less rigorous satellite or alternate campus. You can then evaluate if starting at an alternate campus is a good plan for you, and ask if transferring to the main campus is an option later on. Attaining high "freshman retention," ensuring freshman come back for their second year, is an important goal for colleges. Admitting you on a conditional basis may help you stay on track for your freshman year, and if you are doing well in college, you can complete your conditional terms of acceptance and move on from there.

ACCEPTANCE

An acceptance is what you've been aiming for during the college admissions process. It is a time for celebration of your hard work during high school!

WAITLIST

A waitlist notification from a college means you are being seriously considered for admission but you have to wait until late spring or summer to be notified of a final decision. More information about what "being waitlisted" means and how to handle this is covered later in the chapter.

I've been accepted to several colleges; how do I decide which one to attend?

You may have thought you were done with the hard part when you sent out your last college application. However, if you receive letters of acceptance from more than one school, you still have a very important decision to make.

> *"Success and happiness at an institution are ultimately more about finding a good match than about institutional rankings or brand names. The gut feeling you get after a campus visit is a useful indicator of that potential match. Don't ignore it.*
>
> *Students learn in different ways, and the college experience will be significantly different from any high school experience, even for the most dedicated students. For institutions of choice on your short list, try to get a sense of what the learning experience will be like before making a final commitment; talk with current students, alums, and even faculty members."*
>
> —Nancy Maly, Director of Admission, Grinnell College

To sum it all up, you need to look at several factors to help you decide which college to attend and then ask yourself the following:

- Which college meets most of my needs?
- What do my parents/close family think?
- What do my friends/peers think?
- What are the economic ramifications of choosing each college?
- Did I get the right vibe (the "X" factor)?

There is no one "best fit" college for everyone. There are probably many colleges which would best meet your needs. The most important predictor of future success is how well you do in college, not necessarily which college you attend. Some students make decisions logically, others make decisions based on their feelings; both are valuable tools in making a choice. Go back and take a look at the list of criteria in Chapter 3 for a review of how you evaluated your potential college choices.

We all know how important your family members are in the college admissions process, and they are even more important when it comes to selecting which college to attend. Talk to your family, and ask them for their recommendations and the reasons for their choice. A family's influence is a critical factor in the decision-making process.

Some of you may place a very high premium on where your friends and even your acquaintances will be attending college. Do you want to have at least one friend with you in college? Do you want to attend college with many friends, or do you want to be the pioneer who branches away from the pack? The only caution here is that you need to do what's right for you and not just follow other people's lead. Now is the time to be an independent thinker, so ultimately you should do what's in your best interest.

Economic factors may be a prime factor in your final decision. You may need to choose a financially affordable college, which also meets your other needs. In times of economic distress, economic factors are a reality which you may not want to address but you need to face. Decisions can be delayed until March or April, when you receive your financial aid packets from most of your colleges, so you can compare aid packages as discussed in Chapter 7. Students in all income levels need to take into account the financial reality of their situation when making a final choice.

> *"Do your due diligence on each of your choices. Leave aside the opinions of friends and family and try to determine where you will be happiest and most successful. If you need to, go back and visit each campus, but this time make sure that you view it not through the can-I-get-in lens, but through the do-I-want-to-study-and-live-here-for-four-years lens. Many students report that campus visits in April (after getting acceptances) were the determining factor in their college choice."*
>
> –Paul Marthers, EdD, Dean of Admission, Reed College

> *"When looking at colleges, you need to narrow down your choice and try to picture yourself in each setting. Where do you feel most comfortable? Visit any college that you're seriously thinking of attending—don't rely on what you've heard or think you know. Spend some time exploring the campus, talk with students, sit in on a class, go to the library, see the surrounding towns. Students also generally start a Facebook site for the 'incoming class of XX'; join those and see how you relate to the other students who are seriously thinking of going there. As one student said, 'I knew Quinnipiac was the place for me because I thought I'd be okay if my parents got in the car and drove away.' Find that place for you."*
>
> –Joan Mohr, VP and Dean of Admissions, Quinnipiac University

Once you receive your offers of acceptance, visiting for a second time is always a good idea. Don't discount the "X" factor when deciding between colleges. Many colleges host "accepted student days," where you can meet other students and professors in your projected major. You may also want to participate in an overnight campus visit to get a feel for what it would be like to live there.

What is the universal reply date?

When you make a final decision, you must inform the one college you will be attending by May 1. May 1st is referred to as the "universal reply date," because that is the agreed upon date for colleges throughout the country to receive decisions from students. May 1st is usually a postmark date, the date by which you must mail your response. This date does not apply if you have applied and been accepted to your early decision school. You are not required to respond to colleges before May 1st under any other admission plans.

> If you receive an acceptance letter from a college and they ask you to send your decision along with a deposit by a date earlier than May 1, the college may be in violation of NACAC's Principles of Good Practices. Colleges which ask for an earlier reply date must offer you the chance to extend your reply date in writing to May 1. If you have difficulties with any college regarding an extension of your reply date, you can file a complaint with your guidance counselor or you can notify NACAC directly:
>
> **National Association of College Admissions Counselors**
> 1050 N. Highland Street, Suite 400
> Arlington, VA 22201
> 800-822-6285 or 703-836-2222

It is also required that you notify colleges which you have decided not to attend. Many students forget to do this, but it is your responsibility to notify all colleges, so your spot in the freshman class is available to another student who may be on a waitlist. As you may also be waitlisted at a college, it is common courtesy and expected of students to notify all colleges of your intended plans.

You can notify colleges you do not wish to attend by returning a reply form you should have received with your acceptance letter, or you can just write a short letter to the colleges' Office of Admissions. A sample letter you can use is as follows:

Date

College Name

Address

Dear Admissions Officer:

Thank you for your offer of admission for fall _____. I have decided to attend another university, <u>(name of university-optional)</u>, so I will not be accepting your offer.

Sincerely,

(sign your name here)

Name

ID #

ENROLLMENT FORM AND DEPOSIT

Along with returning your "intent to enroll" form, you may also be asked to send an enrollment deposit as well as a housing deposit. If you plan to take a gap year, check with your college to determine if you need to send any deposit at this time or if you can wait a few months. You can only send a deposit to *one* college. The only exception to this practice is if you are waitlisted at a college you are seriously considering. Many students do not realize you are not allowed to "double deposit," which is sending a deposit to more than one college.

Many students and their families believe they are not harming anyone by double depositing. The concept of double depositing goes against NACAC's Principles of Ethical Practices, which students, counselors, and colleges are expected to follow. If a college finds out you have double deposited, your offer of acceptance could be withdrawn by *both* colleges. There are rules of conduct which everyone involved in the college admissions process needs to follow, and this practice is certainly one you should be aware of.

Should I take a gap year? If so, how do I defer my acceptance?

A gap year is a post high school experience where you can engage in research, work, volunteer, travel, or participate in other opportunities. If you are admitted to a college and you want to take a gap year, you must request a deferral from that college to reserve your place until the following year.

There are several benefits of taking a gap year. It can serve as an opportunity to:

- Obtain valuable life experience
- Gain maturity and perspective
- Focus on a potential major/career
- Save money for college
- Re-apply to a college or program to which you weren't originally accepted, as long as you didn't accept another college's offer

Colleges generally look favorably on gap year experiences. Some universities, including Harvard and Princeton, encourage their students to participate in a gap year. Princeton began a pilot "Bridge Year" program with students accepted for fall 2009. Interested students who were accepted into the program will participate in the tuition-free program. Students spend nine months overseas engaging in community service projects. If successful, the program will be expanded for future classes.

The policies for granting deferrals vary widely from college to college. You should check on a school's policy before you request a deferral. You also need to find out whether any scholarships or special program acceptances, including Honors programs, will be honored or whether you will be re-evaluated with next year's pool of applicants. If a college does not defer acceptances, you may need to re-activate your application or re-apply with a new application. Check with your prospective colleges about their policy.

The process for requesting a deferral involves completing a "deferral request form," if a college has one, or writing a letter to the Admissions Office. A sample letter looks like this:

Date

College Name

Address

Dear Admissions Officer:

Thank you for your offer of admission. I would like to request a one year deferral to participate in the <u>name of program</u>.

I look forward to attending <u>name of college</u> in fall _____. Thank you for your consideration of my request.

Sincerely,

Name

ID#

Once your request is submitted, you should receive a response from your college indicating if your request was accepted. You should also receive instructions about whether you need to re-activate your application or re-apply, or whether your spot will be held for you. If you have any questions, you should ask the Office of Admissions.

The Gap Year: A Sampling of College Policies and Views

"A student admitted for a particular year may request deferral for one year. They must write to us and outline their reasons for requesting deferral, as well as their plan for the interim year. If the plan is determined worthwhile, we would approve it, but that is not guaranteed. Deferrals are granted for one year only and the student must agree not to apply to other colleges or enroll elsewhere during the interim year."—Lorne Robinson, Dean of Admissions and Financial Aid, Macalester College

"For us, students usually go through the application process, and once admitted they ask for a gap year and tell us what their plans are. They may travel, they may work—the only restriction is they can't take classes—otherwise they've become a transfer student, and the process is different. For the gap year student, we hold all their information and reactivate their file during the following year's application process and they're sent a new packet of acceptance information. That gap year can change their whole direction, or can provide a needed change of pace, or can reaffirm exactly what they thought they wanted to do."—Joan Mohr, VP and Dean of Admissions, Quinnipiac University

"At Reed College we find that gap year students arrive with greater maturity and focus. We never discourage admitted students from taking a gap year. I have never met a student for whom a gap year was not a wholly positive experience."—Paul Marthers, EdD, Dean of Admission, Reed College

There are many gap year programs out there. The costs for these programs vary from no fee to costs comparable to one year in college. To ensure you are approved for a gap year, you can provide sufficient information about the program in your deferral request letter. You may have a better chance of being approved if the gap program you choose is an established program. You can start your research by reviewing the following programs:

Name of Program	Web Site/Description
African Leadership Academy	www.alagapyear.org—A 10-month program in South Africa where students choose a service project
Americorps	www.americorps.org—Students participate in service projects in the U.S. and are offered a living allowance and sometimes housing

continued

Name of Program	Web Site/Description
Audubon	www.audubon.org—Offers various opportunities to volunteer or participate in programs in different locations
Brown Ledge	www.brownledgegapyear.com—Students travel to various cities in the U.S., participating in service projects and producing their own documentary about their experiences
Camp Hill Association	www.camphill.org—Participants assist people with developmental disabilities in 1 of 10 Camp Hill communities in North America
Center for Interim Programs	www.interimprograms.com—A fee-based consulting program which matches you with an appropriate gap year experience
City Year	www.cityyear.org—Students participate in 1 of 18 cities, mostly in the U.S., serving as tutors and mentors, working in after-school programs, or leading youth programs
Dynamy Program	www.dynamy.org—An experiential, residential internship program
Enrichment Alley	www.EnrichmentAlley.com—Provides information and links to various gap year programs
Global Quest	www.gquest.org—Offers 12-week programs in Thailand and Ecuador, where students engage in field work, excursions, internships, and service work
Global Service	www.globalservicecorps.org—Offers various overseas service learning programs, including teaching English, AIDS prevention, and international health
Institute for International Cooperation & Development	www.iicd-volunteer.org—Volunteers engage in service projects in Africa, Central America, and Brazil
LeapNow	www.leapnow.org/index.php—A multi-faceted 9-month program in various countries, which includes travel, service projects, and internships
MASA Israel	www.masaisrael.org—A clearinghouse organization providing over 150 opportunities to spend a semester or a year in Israel
National Outdoor Leadership School	www.NOLS.edu—Offers a variety of wilderness and outdoor experiential programs
Outward Bound	www.outwardbound.org—Offers a variety of wilderness and outdoor expeditions in the U.S., Caribbean, and South America

Name of Program	Web Site/Description
Planet Gap Year	www.planetgapyear.com—Provides a database of gap year experiences in the U.S. and overseas
Projects Abroad	www.projects-abroad.org—Participants can volunteer, teach, or engage in archaeology projects in Africa, Asia, Eastern Europe, Latin America, and the South Pacific
Rustic Pathways	www.rusticpathways.com—Participants can choose from a variety of programs or customize their own gap year program in various countries
School of Everything	www.schoolofeverything.com—A social learning network where you can find courses and teachers for every topic
Seamester	www.seamester.com—Offers academic and adventure voyages at sea, where participants learn about oceanography, marine biology, sailing, and leadership
Semester At Sea	www.semesteratsea.org—Offers voyages at sea, investigating new cultures, lands, and people in a variety of locations
ServeNet	www.servenet.org—Offers a variety of volunteer opportunities worldwide
The Gap Year Advantage	gapyearadvantage.com—A book offering advice for planning and implementing a gap year
Thinking Beyond Borders	www.thinkingbeyondborders.org—A 35-week program offering a variety of service learning opportunities in multiple locations in the U.S. and overseas
Where There Be Dragons	www.wheretherebedragons.com—Offers a variety of experiential programs in various international locations, fostering cross-cultural education, global citizenship, and community action
World Learning	www.worldlearning.org—Operates international education and development programs in 70 countries

What happens if I get waitlisted?

One possible outcome when hearing back from colleges is that you have been waitlisted. Being placed on a waitlist is a positive occurrence, because it is preferable to a rejection. If you are waitlisted at a college of your choice, it means you are a serious contender for a spot in the freshman class, but you were not able to be admitted because all of the initial spots have been filled. Remember, the goal of most colleges is to have a full freshman class so they don't lose money.

However, more spots may open up once students have responded by the Universal Reply Date of May 1st. At that time, many colleges will go to their waitlist. Since colleges do not know until May 1st how many freshman seats are available, the number of students on a waitlist and the number of students taken off the waitlist vary from college to college and from year to year.

> *"Getting a waitlist letter can be depressing and can make you even more anxious, especially if it's from that special college that you're hoping to attend. But being on a waitlist doesn't mean you won't eventually get in. My advice is to let the college know that you're interested (most provide a way to 'reply' to being waitlisted), but do so only if that college is your first or second choice. Don't try to rack up admits just to say you were admitted. Let another student move forward on the waitlist if you feel you wouldn't attend even if you were admitted later on. Students can provide midyear grades, any new information that's relevant, and if it's really their first choice—yes, let them know that. And I recommend that the student, not the parent, should call the college. If you're taken off the waitlist and offered acceptance, most colleges will expect that you're at least 50 percent likely to attend."*
>
> –Joan Mohr, VP and Dean of Admissions, Quinnipiac University

The chances of being accepted from a waitlist can be unpredictable. According to the Rice University Web site, the number of students offered admission from the waitlist in 2007 was six students. In 2006, 110 students were offered admission from the waitlist. As you can see, it is very hard to predict how many students will be accepted from the waitlist every year.

When you are placed on a waitlist, you will be asked if you want to remain on the waitlist. You can remain on more than one college's waitlist, and you should not be asked for a deposit or a commitment until you have been officially notified of an acceptance. You will need to reply to a waitlist offer by a certain date. If you have already been accepted to your first choice school or if you are happy with the schools you have been accepted to, you can decline the waitlist offer. If, however, you are not happy with the schools you have been accepted to or the school to which you are waitlisted is one of your top choices, then you should accept the waitlist offer. If you remain on a waitlist, you should go ahead and accept one other school's offer and send the required deposit by May 1st. If you are eventually admitted to your waitlist college and you want to attend, then you must withdraw from the school you originally accepted and go ahead and accept the waitlisted school's offer. This is the only situation where you can double deposit, and you will most likely lose your deposit to the first school.

There really is no downside to being waitlisted, except that you are in limbo for a while and there is some uncertainty as to where you are going to college. You will start hearing from your waitlisted schools in May and June, and you should be notified no later than August 1.

> *"Reed always maintains a waiting list. Each of the seven years I have worked at Reed, the College has admitted students from the waiting list—sometimes as few as 14; other times as many as 40. As soon as they receive notification of the waitlist decision, waitlisted students should tell the admission office (in writing) that they wish to be 'live' prospects on the waiting list; in other words, tell the college that you will enroll if admitted. Most selective colleges encourage waitlisted applicants to send supplemental materials that might strengthen the case for admission. In the last week of April, those students who are still very interested in getting admitted should write or call the admission office again to convey that strong interest. Most admission offices want to make admission offers to waitlisted students who will accept that offer. Conversely, if you are no longer interested in the college, let it know so the admission staff there can concentrate on students still hanging on hoping for an admit offer."*
>
> *–Paul Marthers, EdD, Dean of Admission, Reed College*

Many students wonder if waitlisted students are ranked in order of their number on the waitlist, but that is not the case. The applications of waitlisted students are typically reviewed again. Whether you are accepted depends on how a college is building their freshman class and what their needs (academic, sports, etc.) are for that incoming class. You can increase your chances of being accepted from a waitlist by:

- Maintaining your senior grades
- Updating your file through a letter or e-mail, expressing your most recent accomplishments and your continued interest in the college
- Writing a new essay
- Obtaining a new letter of recommendation from a senior teacher or someone else
- Planning a return visit to the campus and expressing your interest
- Continuing a dialogue with your admissions representative through e-mail
- Considering alternate admissions terms, such as a guaranteed transfer (you will be admitted as a transfer student if you meet certain GPA requirements), an alternate semester, or an alternate campus

> *"Yes, like most selective colleges, we offer some students a place on our Alternate List every year. These are students we'd love to enroll if we have more room. Later (after the May 1 reply date), we may find that we have space to offer admission to some of these students and will review those applications again at that time. Who ends up being admitted often depends on how the enrolling class is shaping up at that time. Waitlisted students should keep their files up to date by submitting additional transcripts or updated activity/award information when available."*
>
> *–Lorne Robinson, Dean of Admissions and Financial Aid, Macalester College*

Do senior grades count?

After reviewing your final high school transcript, we are disappointed in the decline of your senior grades. Our offer of admission was contingent upon your satisfactory completion of your senior year course load. We are concerned about your commitment to academic excellence. Therefore, we are taking the following action....

If you are the recipient of the above letter, it means you have caught a dreaded disease, senioritis. The emphatic answer to the question about whether senior grades count is yes! If you do not take your senior classes seriously, you may be notified by your college that you have not fulfilled your end of the bargain. An offer of acceptance is always a conditional one, with the expectation that you will satisfactorily complete your senior courses. The definition of satisfactory completion varies from college to college and from student to student. If you are a 90 student, your grades should not dip below the middle to upper 80's. If you are an 80 student, your grades should not fall below the middle to upper 70's. If you drop more than five points, you may receive a "disappointed letter."

Many seniors wrongly perceive senior year as a time to goof off and enjoy their remaining time in high school. High school is four years, not three as some seniors believe, so you must continue to focus on senior year courses. Your college acceptance may be in jeopardy, so do not ignore the warning signs, such as:

- Phone calls or letters sent home from your teachers
- Increase in unexcused absences
- Drop in grades

Do not underestimate the seriousness of this problem. There are several potential actions which colleges can take:

- Withdraw or rescind an offer of acceptance
- Ask you to call or write with an explanation of your decline in grades
- Place you on academic probation
- Withdraw scholarship money
- Require regular meetings with academic advisors or a dean

Keep in mind colleges are first receiving your final transcript in the end of June or in July, so you may not receive a "disappointed" letter until late July or August. At this point, you would have told everyone where you are going to college, and you will be preparing to begin classes soon. You will have to immediately respond to a letter if you get one. You must explain your behavior, and you should be legitimately sorry and accept responsibility for your actions. If you are fortunate, colleges may accept your apology and permit you to attend their college in the fall, if you agree to the conditions they impose on you. If you have completely bombed your senior year and your offer is rescinded, you may have to make a major change in plans and attend an alternate college at the last minute. Do not let senioritis happen to you, as the consequences may be very severe and embarrassing. Fortunately, you can avoid this scenario. You have been forewarned, so take all of your senior classes seriously.

What Admissions Counselors Say About "Senioritis"

To give you an idea of the gravity of senioritis, our admissions counselors impart their policies about senior grades:

"Students need to stay on track during senior year. They need to avoid a grade slump and also avoid the tendency to take a lighter course load in the senior year. The most selective colleges put a premium on the senior schedule and grades earned, because senior courses are usually the ones that offer the best preparation for college courses.

Senior grades definitely count. When looking at regular cycle applicants, selective colleges always pay attention to senior grades. And selective colleges often check on 7th semester grades when reviewing early decision applicants.

In general, the more selective the college, the more likely it is that all high school grades matter."–Paul Marthers, EdD, Dean of Admission, Reed College

"No final decisions are made without first or second quarter senior grades. If an admitted student receives a senior year grade which is dramatically out of line with previous grades, the student is contacted to find out what is happening. It would be unlikely, barring extraordinary circumstances, that someone with a senior year D or F grade would be admitted without a plausible explanation."–Nancy Maly, Director of Admission, Grinnell College

"Yes, senior grades count. They count heavily. All colleges will require a copy of your final high school transcript. We are looking to see that you are a dedicated, committed student. Students who catch 'senior-it is' and begin to take their work less seriously are indicating that once they get to our campuses, they may do the same thing. I have seen offers of admission rescinded. Remember, getting accepted is not the end goal. Earning your college degree is the end goal...you can't let up."–Jacquelyn Nealon, VP Enrollment Services, New York Institute of Technology

---

In addition to poor grades in senior year, there are other reasons why a college may withdraw its offer after you have been accepted:

- False information or statements on your application
- Disciplinary issues, including violence, cheating, drug-related charges, theft, and inappropriate Web posting
- Sending multiple deposits to colleges

You've worked so hard to gain acceptance to college, don't risk having an offer withdrawn by violating the above ethical principles. These violations were discussed in Chapter 6; for more information, consult NACAC's "Students' Rights and Responsibilities in the College Admission Process" in Appendix E.

What are my senior year responsibilities?

As we have previously discussed, the senior year is of critical importance to colleges. As a senior in high school, you still have much to do. Your responsibilities include:

- Ensuring your applications are complete and all documents have been received by your colleges (you can use the "Tracking Applications Checklist" in Chapter 6 to assist you)
- Thanking teachers and counselors for writing letters of recommendation (a sincere thank-you note or a small token of appreciation is appropriate)
- Re-visiting colleges once you have been accepted in order to make your final decision
- Ensuring your parents file the FAFSA and other financial aid documents as soon as possible after January 1 (discussed in Chapter 7)
- Considering obtaining a job to help you pay for college
- Researching potential scholarships you may qualify for and getting applications in on time (check Chapter 7 and Appendix B for sample scholarships)
- Researching and planning a gap year, if possible (covered earlier in this chapter)
- Planning for something to do the summer before you enter college: job, internship, volunteer, travel, research
- Reviewing the general education or core requirements needed for the college you will be attending
- Preparing for college—attending orientations, registering for classes, and shopping for dorm and other needed items

How do I deal with rejection?

Dealing with rejection of any type is not easy. If you are rejected from your first-choice college or any other colleges, allow yourself a little time to feel sad or disappointed, but don't dwell on it. The best way to get over a setback is to focus on what you can do about it, which is to move forward. Here are some ways:

- Go back and visit colleges you may have initially ruled out.
- Focus on other colleges you are still waiting to hear from.

- Apply to a few more colleges. As we discussed in Chapter 9, there are many colleges with later deadlines.

- Think about taking a gap year and trying again to apply to a wider range of colleges. I know one student who was disappointed that he was not accepted to some highly selective colleges. He took a gap year doing something he was very passionate about, taking classes in music. He then reapplied the following year to a number of highly competitive colleges, and he was accepted to several of these schools.

It really pays to know what you want, to pursue your passion, and to persevere. Staying positive, doing what you love, and knowing how to communicate this excitement to colleges can sometimes lead to a second look by colleges. Also, you can attend a "safety" school you really like, and if you are truly not happy there, you can transfer. Many students transfer to another college during their college career, and it is the college you graduate from that really counts, not the college where you began. As long as you realize there are always options, you will be able to recover from your initial rejection.

I've been accepted! Now what?

Now that you've been accepted, sent in your deposit, and avoided senioritis, you can focus on next year. You will either be engaging in a gap year experience or heading to college. College is a time of discovery and exploration.

Before you begin college, most colleges offer an orientation session in the summer to familiarize you with the campus and give you an opportunity to meet your peers. Some orientations are held weeks or months before classes begin, and others are held right before the semester starts. To help you adjust to college life, Joan Mohr, VP and Dean of Admissions at Quinnipiac University, recommends that you "bring photos with you to college of your friends, pets, family, and favorite memories. You'll want to share them with your roommates, and you'll want to have them surrounding you. Often there may be a common reading for the incoming class—and taking a few notes as you go through it will help you remember what you read when you get to your new situation. If you haven't been diligent about learning to do laundry or how a bank account works, start now. You'll be asked to solve your own problems—and with your parents just a phone call away, you'll be tempted to call and ask them to solve them for you. College is about gaining independence and learning to trust yourself and your decisions. Yes, you'll take some lumps and you'll make some mistakes, and that's okay. Seek help when you need it. Don't be afraid to ask—and realize all those other incoming students are just as nervous as you are. Getting *into* college has been your focus, now it's time to make *graduating* from college your goal."

Many colleges are concerned that some freshmen may not succeed in college, because they are used to being told what to do by their parents and teachers. Some colleges require that freshmen participate in special freshman seminars, which teach students how to use the library and other resources offered by the college, including counseling services. Jacquelyn Nealon, VP of Enrollment Services at New York Institute of Technology, addresses one of the areas of concern for freshmen. "One of the biggest adjustments for incoming freshmen is the amount of autonomy they will have in terms of budgeting their time. Think about how you will manage your time. How will you schedule study time? Work out an academic and study plan that you can follow. Brush up on writing and communication skills."

How can we sum up the admissions process?

The college admissions process is an exciting yet demanding process. If you are proactive and do extensive research, you will be rewarded with a college choice that is a good fit for you. If you have made some mistakes along the way or did things at the last minute, you can still recover and land in a school just right for you. The good news is there are always options.

As you go through the admissions process and talk to your family about it, just be aware that the process has changed in the last several decades. Some of these changes were discussed in the Introduction and they will impact admissions in the next decade. The admissions landscape is changing and evolving, and continues to do so. There are demographic shifts, increases in the minority population, and an existing gender gap. There is a testing frenzy, with an over-reliance on standardized test scores. Some colleges are reacting to this frenzy by moving away from standardized test scores and placing less emphasis on them. There are economic realities, which students and colleges need to face. Some students may alter their plans to cut college costs by attending financially affordable schools; colleges may need to tighten their belts by offering fewer courses or programs. The best way to handle the uncertainty in the process is to use all of the resources at your disposal to make an educated decision once you hear from all of your colleges.

Let's take a last look at an overview of the admissions process and hopefully you will be successful in navigating your way through the college application process. A first and critical step before you begin the application process is to define who you are. This step can be accomplished by conducting a self-assessment (Chapter 1). Gathering information includes using all of the resources available to you to identify what criteria you should consider when researching colleges (Chapter 3). You generate a list of prospective colleges by visiting campuses (Chapter 4) and identifying a range of colleges which fit your needs. The application process consists of the application itself (Chapter 6) as well as supplementary materials, including transcripts, standardized tests, essays, extracurricular activities, and financial aid (covered in chapters 2, 5, 6, and 7). When you are notified of a decision by colleges, you are ready to evaluate your choices and make a decision. The last step involves fulfilling your responsibilities as a senior and getting ready for college (covered in this chapter).

Any final suggestions?

As you near the end of the college admissions process, you should realize that there are many colleges which fit your academic, social, and financial needs. College is the means to an end and—as Jacquelyn Nealon, VP of Enrollment Services at New York Institute of Technology, asserts, "College is a marathon, not a sprint. The undergraduate degree is just the first leg in a longer race. It's not the end point. So, try not to put so much emphasis on making the 'right' choice. At the end of the day, it's the college education that is the critical tool needed in the tool-belt for life-long success."

Many admissions officers recommend you start the process early and not wait until the beginning of senior year to begin the thought process and planning required in applying to college. Cheryl Brown, Director of Undergraduate Admissions at Binghamton University, suggests that you not "narrow your college choices too soon. Look at both big and small schools, both schools close to home and far away, and both public and private. Visit during your junior year. Make second visits to your top choices in the fall of senior year as you are going through the application process."

The application process cannot be quantified and in many ways is unpredictable. It is not an art and it is not a science. Raymond Lutzky, Director of Outreach at Rensselaer Polytechnic Institute, sums up the process by saying, "students get into some schools for the craziest of reasons, and others will not get into their top choice for reasons that may not be clear. Nevertheless, students should remember that when dealing with selective colleges, they will visit a few that they like, they will get into some, and then make a decision as to where to go. Everyone gets in 'somewhere,' but often students are left with fears from 'musical chairs' in early childhood. No student is left with a stack of rejection letters and 'no chair' at the end of the music."

Appendix

A

Web Sites

The following Web sites can be useful during all phases of the college admissions process. You can use these sites to search for college matches, potential careers, financial aid, jobs, and scholarships. You can also find information about centralized applications and standardized testing.

College Applications

www.commonapp.org
www.universalcollegeapp.com
www.questbridge.org

College Search Web Sites

www.college.gov
www.nces.ed.gov/ipeds/cool
www.cappex.com
www.admissions.com
www.nacanet.org
www.CollegeClickTV.com
www.collegeconfidential.com
www.mycollegeoptions.org
www.campustours.com
www.ecampustours.com
www.unigo.com
www.gocollege.com
www.campusexplorer.com

www.collegebound.net
www.findtherightschool.com
www.collegenet.com
www.collegeview.com
www.anycollege.com

Careers

www.Online.onetcenter.org
- Federal government Web site
- Career information
- Links and online resources

www.careervoyages.gov
- Federal government Web site
- Links to career/college resources in each state

www.nycareerzone.org
- New York State Web site for high school students
- Link to "The Interest Profiler"
- Career search/links to college
- Resume developer

www.iseek.org
- Minnesota Web site for students
- Career information
- Education information, job information

www.ioscar.org/tx
- Texas Web site for students
- Occupation and skill center

www.humanmetrics.com
- Free Myers Briggs Type Indicator Personality assessment

www.careeronestop.org

www.HealthManagementCareers.org

www.bls.gov/oco

Financial Aid

www.fafsa.ed.gov

www.collegesavings.org

www.students.gov

www.FederalStudentAid.ed.gov

http://wdcrobcolp01.ed.gov/Programs/EROD/org_list.cfm?category_ID=SHE

www.nasfaa.org

www.studentaid.ed.gov

http://fafsademo.test.ed.gov

www.upromise.com

www.nasfaa.org/Redesign/TaxBenefitsguide.html

Jobs

http://gottajob.com

www.groovejob.com

www.teens4hire.org

Scholarships

www.fastweb.com

www.meritaid.com

www.wiredscholar.com

www.finaid.org

www.csocollegecenter.org

www.thesalliemaefund.org/smfnew/scholarship/first_family.html

www.collegeanswer.com

www.americorps.org

www.hhs.gov/grants/index.shtml#education

www.goarmy.com/benefits/education.jsp

www.navy.com/benefits/education

www.airforce.com/opportunities/enlisted/education

www.marines.com/main/index/quality_citizens/benefit_of_service/education

www.bbb.com

www.StudentScholarshipSearch.com

ww5.komen.org/Content.aspx?id=6504

www.ncte.org/awards/student/aa

www.spj.org/a_hs.asp

www.hsf.net

www.teachforamerica.org

www.peacecorps.gov

Testing

www.act.org

www.collegeboard.com

www.ibo.org

Appendix

B

National Scholarships

The following list is a sample of national scholarships for which you can apply; it is not a complete list. You can also check Appendix A for scholarship search and financial aid Web sites.

Scholarship	Eligibility	Award	Web Site
CAREER-RELATED			
American Chemical Society	Minority students with interest in chemistry	Up to $5,000	www.chemistry.org/scholars
DECA (Business)	DECA member	Varies	www.deca.org/schol.html
National Association of Hispanic Journalists	Interest in journalism	Varies	www.nahj.org/educationalprograms/currentscholarships.Shtml
National Institutes of Health Undergraduate Scholarship Program	3.5 GPA or top 5% in class, disadvantaged background, interested in careers in biomedical/science	Up to $20,000	https://ugsp.nih.gov/home.asp?m=00
Society of Women Engineers Scholarship	Women, interest in engineering	$1,000–10,000	www.swe.org/stellent/idcplg?IdcService=SS_GET_PAGE&nodeId=9
Xerox Technology Minority Scholarship	3.0 GPA, minority, interest in chemistry, physics, material science, engineering	$1,000–10,000	www.xerox.com/go/xrx/template/009.jsp?ed_name=Careers_Technical_Scholarship&view=Feature

continued

Scholarship	Eligibility	Award	Web Site
CORPORATE			
Best Buy	Good grades, Community service	1,000 awards of $1,500	www.bestbuyinc.com/community_relations/scholarship.htm
Coca-Cola	3.0 GPA, leadership & extracurricular activities	50 awards of $20,000; 200 awards of $10,000	www.coca-colascholars.org
Dell Scholars	Need based, 2.4 GPA, participate in college readiness program	$20,000	www.dellscholars.org/public
Discover	2.75 GPA, community service/leadership	10 awards of $30,000	www.discoverfinancial.com/community/scholarship.shtml
Duck Brand Duct Tape "Stick at Prom"	Original prom attire	$1,000–3,000	www.ducktapeclub.com
Financial Service Centers of America (FiSCA)	Academic, leadership, overcoming obstacles	$2,000+	www.fisca.org/Content/NavigationMenu/CommunityOutreach/FiSCANationalScholarshipProgram/default.htm
Kohl's Kids Who Care	Community service	$1,000–Regional; $5,000–National	www.Kohlscorporation.com/CommunityRelations/scholarship/Index.asp
Prudential Spirit of Community Award	Community service	$1,000–State winners; $5,000–National winners	spirit.prudential.com/view/page
Sallie Mae Fund Scholarship Programs	Various programs	Varies	www.thesalliemaefund.org/smfnew/scholarship/index.html
Scholar Athlete Milk Mustache of the Year (SAMMY)	Sports, academic, leadership, community service	$7,500	www.bodybymilk.com/sammy
Signet Classics Scholarship Essay Contest	Essay contest	$1,000	us.penguingroup.com/static/pages/services-academic/essayhome.html
UPromise Scholarship	3.0 GPA, financial need	$2,500	www.scholarshipamerica.org/upromise

Scholarship	Eligibility	Award	Web Site
FOUNDATIONS/UNIONS			
Davidson Fellows	Completed works in literature, music, math, technology, philosophy, outside the box	Up to $50,000	www.davidsongifted.org/fellows
Elks National Foundation Most Valuable Student	Scholarship, financial need, leadership	$1,000–15,000	www.elks.org/enf/scholars/ourscholarships.cfm
Gates Millennium Scholars	3.3 GPA, low income; American Indian, Alaska native, Asian Pacific Islander, African American, Hispanic, Pell Grant eligibility criteria	Amount varies	www.gmsp.org/publicweb/Scholarships.aspx
Gloria Barron Prize for Leadership and Service	Essay contest	$2,000	www.barronprize.org
Holocaust Remembrance Project	Essay contest	Up to $10,000	holocaust.hklaw.com
Horatio Alger	2.0 GPA, financial need, extracurricular activities, community service	Up to $20,000	www.horatioalger.com/scholarships/apply.cfm
Key Club International Scholarship Program	3.0 GPA, member of Key Club	Varies	www.keyclub.org
Union Plus AFL/CIO	Union members	$500–4,000	www.unionplus.org/college-education-financing/union-plusscholarship
Voice of Democracy Veterans of Foreign War	Audio essay	$1,000–30,000	www.vfw.org

continued

Scholarship	Eligibility	Award	Web Site
MINORITY STUDENTS			
Hispanic Scholarship Fund	Various programs	Varies	www.hsf.net
Ron Brown Scholar	Academic, leadership, financial need	$10,000	www.ronbrown.org/home.aspx
The Jackie Robinson Foundation's Scholarship Program	Minority student, financial need, leadership potential	Up to $1,500	www.jackierobinson.org/apply
United Negro College Fund	Various programs	Varies	www.uncf.org/forstudents/scholarship.asp
SCIENCE/TALENT COMPETITIONS			
Intel Science Talent Scholarship	Original research	Up to $100,000	www.societyforscience.org/sts
National Merit Scholarship Program	Based on PSAT scores, notified by high school	Varies	www.nationalmerit.org
Siemens Competition	Math, science & technology research	Up to $100,000	www.siemens-foundation.org/en/competition.htm
SPECIAL SCHOLARSHIPS			
American Cancer Society	Students who have had cancer or currently have cancer	Varies	www.cancer.org/docroot/SPC/content/SPC_1_College_Scholarships_List.asp
Anne Ford Scholarship	3.0 GPA, students with learning disabilities	$10,000	www.ncld.org/content/view/725/508
Cancer Survivors Fund	Students who have had cancer or currently have cancer	Varies	www.cancersurvivorsfund.org

Scholarship	Eligibility	Award	Web Site
Coca-Cola First Generation Scholarship	3.0 GPA, first in family to attend college	Up to $5,000	www.thecoca-colacompany.com/ citizenship/education.html
Komen 5 Scholarship	Loss of a parent due to breast cancer, scholastic achievement, financial need, leadership	Up to $10,000	ww5.komen.org/Content. aspx?id=6504
September 11 Family Members	Family members of 9/11	Varies	www.scholarships.com/ september-11-scholarships. aspx#Aon

Glossary

504 Plan A plan, developed by school professionals under Section 504 of the Rehabilitation Act of the Americans with Disabilities Act, designed to give students with disabilities needed modifications and accommodations.

Achievement Test A test designed to assess information learned in a specific curriculum. The concepts measured are usually content-specific and more factual rather than abstract.

ACT The ACT is one of the tests used to assess college readiness. It is composed of English, reading, math, and science sections and an optional writing section. Each section is scored from 1 to 36 with a composite score from 1 to 36.

Advanced Placement (AP) The Advanced Placement program and tests developed by the College Board. Many high schools offer AP courses and students take AP exams (scored on a scale from 1 to 5) in May for potential college credit. AP courses are usually challenging courses, and colleges look favorably upon students who take them.

Aptitude Test A test designed to measure future potential; the concepts tested are usually more abstract.

Block Schedule A type of course programming used in high schools where classes do not meet every day but meet for longer periods of time a few times a week. One of the benefits of block scheduling is longer class periods with intense focus.

Brag Sheet Also known as an extracurricular activities sheet or a resume, the brag list highlights students' achievements inside and outside of school. *See also Extracurricular Activities List* and *Résumé*.

Campus Visit A trip taken by many students to tour a campus before they apply to determine if the school has the right "vibe" and is a good match for them.

Career Assessment Online or paper and pencil assessments used to measure preferences for certain careers or jobs based on a student's self assessment of his or her personality.

Class Rank A comparative rating measurement used by some high schools to rank students' performance in the senior class, either with a weighted or an unweighted grade point average.

College Admissions Counselor/Officer Professionals who work in the college admissions office of a college or university. They read students' applications and recruit students by visiting high schools and participating in college fairs around the country.

College Level Course These courses are offered in high schools, usually in conjunction with a local college or university. Students may pay lower tuition for these courses and receive college credits when they enter college.

College Level Examination Program (CLEP) A testing program administered by the College Board, which is used to grant college credit in 34 areas.

College Preparatory Classes Courses offered in high school to prepare students for college level work. These courses are usually in English, science, social studies, foreign language, and math.

College Rankings Published rankings of colleges developed by various media, including *US News and World Report, Business Week,* and *Forbes.* Various criteria are used to evaluate colleges.

College Savings Program Various programs used by families to save money for college, including 529 plans and prepaid tuition programs.

Common Application A centralized application for students to use to apply to member colleges that promote holistic review of applications. Students can apply online or on paper.

Common Data Set Statistics provided on a university's Web site, which includes useful information about admissions data.

Community College A two-year college with low tuition, where students can obtain an associate's degree and transfer with credits to a four-year college.

Commuter College Sometimes referred to as a suitcase college, it is a college setting where students typically commute between home and the campus. The college may have dorms for residential students, but most students do not live on campus.

Conditional Acceptance This type of acceptance is granted to students who do not meet the stated requirements of the college but are admitted to college with conditions, including reduced course load, probation, or meetings with academic advisors.

Content-Based Test A test based on the curriculum learned in class. Assessments are objective and students can usually prepare for these tests by reviewing the curriculum.

Co-operative (co-op) Program A program offered by colleges and universities where the emphasis is placed on internships or on-the-job learning experiences.

Core Curriculum Mandatory courses in specific areas or in specific classes students are required to take in order to meet graduation requirements. Some colleges have many core requirements and other colleges have fewer core requirements.

Cost of Attendance (COA) The cost of attending college, including tuition, room and board, travel, personal expenses, books, and fees. The cost of attending a private university is usually higher than that associated with attending a public university.

CSS (College Scholarship Service)/Profile In addition to the FAFSA, some colleges require a more detailed financial aid document known as the CSS/Profile.

Deferred Admission An admission plan where students who apply for early decision but are not offered admission may be moved or deferred to the regular decision pool for another review.

Demonstrated Interest One indicator used by colleges to determine how interested applicants are in enrolling in their college. Demonstrated interest can be assessed through various contacts with the admissions office, including requesting information, campus tours, and contact with the admissions representative.

Double/Multiple Depositing Practice of students sending a deposit to more than one college. According to NACAC's Statement of Ethical Practices, students should send only one deposit to a college by May 1.

Early Action An admission plan where students apply by a college's stated deadline in the fall. Admission decisions are usually given to students in January/February, and students have until May 1 to decide to enroll. Early Action is not a binding commitment.

Early Decision An admission plan where students apply by a college's stated deadline, usually in November or December. Admission decisions are usually given to students in mid December, and the student signs a contract saying they will attend the school if they are accepted. Early Decision is a binding commitment.

Electronic Portfolio Additional application documents that students submit online to a college, including art, creative writing, photos, and other materials.

Expected Family Contribution (EFC) An important number received after completing the FAFSA. The EFC is used to determine what types of financial aid students qualify for.

Extracurricular Activities List Also known as a brag sheet or a resume, this list is used to record students' extracurricular activities and leadership positions. *See also Brag Sheet* and *Résumé.*

Facebook A social networking site on the Web used to communicate with people and to post photos and other personal information. Students need to be careful what they are posting on this site, as prospective colleges and employers periodically scan these Web sites for inappropriate material.

FAFSA (Free Application for Federal Student Aid) A free government online or paper application used to determine students' eligibility for financial aid. The Web site is www.fafsa.ed.gov.

Federal Pell Grant A grant available through the federal government for students who meet the minimum requirements. Pell Grants do not have to be paid back.

Federal Perkins Loans A loan available from the federal government to students who meet minimum requirements. Federal Perkins Loans must be paid back.

Federal PLUS Loans Loans parents can take out to use for college tuition and expenses, which have to be paid back.

Federal Stafford Loans Loans, subsidized and unsubsidized, which students can take out to use for college tuition and expenses. These loans are offered at varying interest rates, and the money borrowed needs to be paid back.

Financial Aid A broad term used to refer to grants, loans, and work study which students may be eligible to receive in order to pay for college and related expenses. Students and/or their families need to complete a FAFSA to determine their eligibility for various federal, state, or college-related programs. *See also FAFSA.*

Financial Aid Package Students receive this package after completing the FAFSA and the CSS/Profile or a college's own financial aid form (if required). A financial aid package describes what funds students will receive from a college to meet college tuition and expenses. Packages will vary by college and may include funds from loans, grants, scholarships, and work study.

Gap Year A year some students take after graduation from high school where they may travel, work, volunteer, study abroad, or conduct research. Most colleges allow students to defer their acceptance for one year in order to participate in worthy gap programs.

Gender Gap A known gap or imbalance in the number of males and females attending college. It is not uncommon to find a female/male ratio of 60 to 40 on many college campuses.

General Education Requirements The minimum requirements needed by students to graduate from college. Some colleges have heavy-duty core requirements, whereas others have fewer mandatory course requirements. These requirements can be checked during the college application process so students are informed about what courses they will need to take in college.

Grade Point Average (GPA) A student's academic average during high school. Some schools use a weighted GPA, where an extra weight is given for honors, college level, IB, or AP courses; other schools use an unweighted average, where all classes are equally weighted.

Grants Grants are a form of financial aid which do not have to be paid back. Grants can be awarded by the federal or state government, or by individual colleges.

Greek Life A term used to describe sorority (girls) or fraternity (boys) life. Some colleges have many students participating in Greek life, while others have few students participating in Greek life.

Guidance Counselor A school professional who counsels students on social, personal, and academic issues, including the college application process.

Highly Likely School Formerly known as a "safety school," a highly likely school is a college where a student has more than the minimum requirements needed to gain admission.

Holistic Approach An approach used by colleges to evaluate whether students will gain admission to their college, including objective (GPA, standardized test scores, difficulty of courses taken) and subjective (essay, letters of recommendation, resume, interview, demonstrated interest) factors.

Honors Program Many colleges offer an honors program for students who have exceeded the minimum requirements needed for admission. Some honors programs offer perks including scholarships, special seminars, laptops, and priority registration.

International Baccalaureate (IB) A rigorous and prestigious program where students take rigorous courses for two years and may receive college credit.

Individual Education Plan (IEP) A plan created by professionals for students with physical and learning disabilities. The plan spells out educational goals, proper placement, and modifications and accommodations needed for the student, which may include extended time, testing in a special location, and use of a computer.

Individuals with Disabilities Education Act (IDEA) A law developed to ensure that students with disabilities receive education and support services. *See also Section 504 Plan.*

Internship A paid or unpaid placement with a professional in an area of interest where the student can learn about the job and gain valuable experience.

Ivy League A group of eight prestigious colleges in the Northeast consisting of Harvard, Princeton, Yale, University of Pennsylvania, Columbia, Brown, Dartmouth, and Cornell. Many families place a high value on these "name brand" colleges.

Learning Disability A neurological disorder that causes difficulty in certain areas. The most common learning disabilities are dyslexia, dyscalculia, dysgraphia, auditory and visual processing disorders, and nonverbal learning disabilities. Support services may be available in college for students who must advocate for themselves.

Legacy Admissions A criterion giving students whose mother or father attended an undergraduate college or university an advantage in the admissions process.

Loans A form of financial aid given to students and/or parents. Loans need to be paid back to the lender, which could be the federal government or a private lender.

Major An area of study selected by a student by the end of their second year of college. Many students enter college with an undecided major; others know what they want to study before they enter college.

Midyear Report Requested by many colleges, this report is used to review midyear grades from seniors to ensure that students are maintaining their academic performance.

Myers Briggs Type Indicator (MBTI) A personality assessment developed by Katharine Briggs and Isabel Briggs Myers based on the works of Carl Jung.

National Association of College Admissions Counselors (NACAC) A national organization for college admissions counselors, guidance counselors, and private consultants which provides research and resources to students, parents, and counselors related to the college admissions process.

National Collegiate Athletic Association (NCAA) An organization which provides information, guidelines, and an eligibility center for student athletes to be recruited by colleges to play competitive sports.

Need The formula for calculating financial need is the Cost of Attendance minus the Expected Family Contribution (EFC), as determined by the FAFSA.

Need Blind A policy used by some colleges where financial need is not taken into account when reviewing students' college applications.

Need Sensitive/Aware A policy used by some colleges where financial need may be taken into account when reviewing students' college applications. Some colleges meet 100 percent of a student's need and other colleges may not meet a student's full need.

Objective Factors Objective factors in the admissions process include GPA, difficulty of courses taken by students, and standardized test scores.

Personal Identification Number (PIN) A number selected or chosen for students and their families when completing a FAFSA. The PIN can be used as an electronic signature on the FAFSA and other documents.

Personal Interview Some colleges offer interviews as one of the subjective factors considered in the admissions process. Interviews may be conducted by admissions officers, alumni, or students.

Personal Statement The long essay on most college applications where students can discuss information not found in the rest of the application. The essay is an opportunity for students to demonstrate their passion and their personality, as well as their fit for a particular college or university.

Priority Application An application with no fee required that is sent to students who have requested information from a college or whose credentials are appealing to a college. It is a way for colleges to increase their pool of applicants.

Private University A school that is privately funded with endowments from alumni and organizations. The cost of tuition is usually higher than at a publicly funded college.

Public Ivy A public university that is highly selective and is ranked just below an Ivy League school. These schools offer great value. Some of the public Ivies are the University of Michigan, University of California at Los Angeles (UCLA), University of North Carolina at Chapel Hill, Binghamton University, and the State University of New York.

Public University Many states have a university system with colleges that are publicly funded, and these schools provide a solid education at a good value.

QuestBridge Application QuestBridge is an application program for highly selective universities with major scholarships offered to qualified candidates with low family incomes. A separate application process is used for this highly selective program.

Reach School A reach or dream school is a highly desirable school, where many applicants have similar qualifications, but not all students can be offered admission. It is highly possible the student may not be accepted for admission, as the competition for spots in the class is fierce.

Regular Decision An admission plan where students apply by a published deadline. Students usually receive a decision by April and have until May 1 to make a decision as to where they will attend college.

Rejection A possible negative outcome when applying to a college or university, especially if students apply to a highly competitive school or to one where their qualifications are below the stated admission requirements.

Rescind A college may withdraw or rescind its offer of admission to students who have not maintained their senior grades or who have had infractions such as lying on the application, cheating, drinking, drugs, double depositing, or other issues. An offer of admission is always contingent upon successful completion of senior year.

Restrictive Early Action An early admission plan where students can apply early action with no commitment to attend, but there are some restrictions on where else you can apply to college. Stanford, Yale, and Boston College are some of the colleges that have some type of restrictions on applying early action.

Résumé A format used to describe extracurricular activities you participate in during high school. It lists your activities, dates involved, positions held, and any honors received.

Rolling Admission A type of admission plan where colleges evaluate applications as they come in. It is suggested that students apply early in the process to these schools, as spaces fill up early and admission standards may be more difficult later in the process.

Room and Board The fees involved in living on campus for a dorm room and a meal plan. These fees are included in the cost of attendance for determining total costs in attending a college.

SAT Reasoning Test A standardized exam covering critical reading, mathematics, and writing, which is required by most colleges as an important tool in the admissions process. The exam is administered by the College Board and each section is scored on a 200–800 point scale.

Scholarships Money given to students by corporations, colleges, and local organizations which does not need to be paid back. Scholarships may be given for academic accomplishments, athletic ability, family background, union membership, or other factors.

School Profile A profile submitted by most high schools to colleges and universities. A school profile contains important information about the high school, including the grading policy, testing results, courses, clubs and organizations offered, and other relevant statistics.

Section 504 Plan A plan developed by a committee of school professionals to provide accommodations to students with disabilities.

Semester A form of scheduling used in many high schools, where students complete two semesters of courses in one year.

Senioritis A widespread feeling that high school is over after three years, where students sometimes do not attend classes or take their coursework seriously during senior year. Students do not realize that these actions can have serious consequences, including having an acceptance withdrawn, being placed on probation, or having to explain your actions.

Standardized Test Scores The SAT and/or the ACT are the two exams required by many colleges in order to compare students' performance in reading, mathematics, writing, and other areas.

Student Aid Report (SAR) A report received by e-mail or by paper about 4–6 weeks after filing a FAFSA. It will include the expected family contribution, which will give students and their families an idea of how much financial aid they can anticipate.

Study Abroad Program Many colleges offer students the opportunity to participate in formal credit-bearing programs overseas. Students may incur extra costs for these programs, and programs should be fully investigated before a commitment is made.

Subject Test The College Board offers one-hour multiple-choice exams, called subject tests, in history, foreign language, math, science, and literature. Some selective colleges require two subject tests. Each exam has a possible score of 200–800. Some colleges will use the ACT as a replacement for subject tests.

Subjective Factors Subjective factors, such as essays, an interview, teacher and counselor letters of recommendation, and extracurricular activities, are examined by colleges using a holistic approach to college admissions.

Supplement Students using the Common Application or the Universal College Application may also need to complete a supplement, which contains specific questions or essays for each college to which they apply.

Target School A college or university which is in the student's target range for GPA, standardized test scores, and other factors. It is a school to which the student is likely to be accepted.

Testing-Optional School There are over 800 colleges or universities which do not require SAT/ACT scores for admission. You can check www.fairtest.org for a list of these schools and their particular requirements.

Transcript One of the most important factors which colleges use to review students' qualifications for admission. The transcript is a record of your high school courses and the grades you received during your freshman, sophomore, and junior years.

Trimester A form of scheduling used by some high schools and colleges, where the student completes three semesters of courses in a year.

Tuition The major cost of attending college. Tuition can be charged per credit, for each semester or trimester, or for the entire school year. Tuition at a private university is usually higher than tuition at a public university.

Universal College Application (UCA) An admissions application used by a consortium of colleges and universities which follow NACAC guidelines. The UCA aims to include many groups of students wishing to apply to colleges online.

Universal Reply Date May 1 is the universal date for students to reply to colleges indicating whether they will accept or decline a college's offer. A form is usually included in students' packets, or students can send a letter with their decision.

Unweighted Average An academic average included on a transcript that does not weight honors, Advanced Placement (AP), college level, or International Baccalaureate (IB) courses.

Waitlist Students may be offered a place on the waitlist when they have qualified for admission but have not been offered a place in the freshman class because of space limitations. When students reply by the Universal Reply Date of May 1, additional spots in the class may become available, and students may be taken off the waitlist and offered admission after May 1.

Weighted Average An academic average included on a transcript that weights courses, such as honors, AP, college level, or IB courses. Some colleges "unweight" a weighted average to compare the average to students in other high schools.

Work Study A form of financial aid where students are given part-time jobs on campus. Students interested in work study can indicate their interest on the FAFSA.

34 Ways to Reduce College Costs

This list is from https://studentaid2.ed.gov/getmoney/pay_for_college/cost_35.html#top:

1. Most colleges and universities offer merit or non-need-based scholarships to academically talented students. Students should check with each school in which they're interested for the criteria for merit scholarships.

2. The National Merit Scholarship Program awards scholarships to students based upon academic merit. The awards can be applied to any college or university to meet educational expenses at that school.

3. Many states offer scholarship assistance to academically talented students. Students should obtain the eligibility criteria from their state's education office.

4. Many schools offer scholarships to athletically talented students. Parents and students should be careful, however, to weigh the benefits of an athletic scholarship against the demands of this type of award.

5. Some colleges and universities offer special grants or scholarships to students with particular talents. Music, journalism, and drama are a few categories for which these awards are made.

6. A state college or university charges lower fees to state residents. Since public institutions are subsidized by state revenues, their tuition costs are lower than private schools' costs. The college selection process should include consideration of a state school. Although cost should be a consideration, students should not base their choice of a school only on cost.

7. Some students choose to attend a community college for 1 or 2 years, and then transfer to a 4-year school. Tuition costs are substantially lower at community colleges than at 4-year institutions.

8. Some parents may be financially able to purchase a house while their child is in school. If other students rent rooms in the house, the income may offset monthly mortgage payments. Families should make certain, however, that the property they purchase meets all of the requirements of rental property. If you have any questions, consult a tax professional.

9. Commuting is another way for students to reduce college costs. A student living at home can save as much as $6,000 per year.

10. Many schools provide lists of housing opportunities that provide free room and board to students in exchange for a certain number of hours of work each week.

11. Co-operative education programs allow students to alternate between working full time and studying full time. This type of employment program is not based upon financial need, and students can earn as much as $7,000 per year.

12. Another way to reduce college costs is to take fewer credits. Students should find out their school's policy regarding the Advanced Placement Program (APP), the College-Level Examination Program (CLEP), and the Provenience Examination Program (PEP). Under these programs, a student takes an examination in a particular subject and, if the score is high enough, receives college credit.

13. Some colleges give credit for life experiences, thereby reducing the number of credits needed for graduation. Students should check with the college for further information. You can also write to Distance Education and Training Council at 1601 18th Street, NW, Washington, DC 20009, or call (202) 234-5100.

14. Most schools charge one price for a specific number of credits taken in a semester. If academically possible, students should take the maximum number of credits allowed. This strategy reduces the amount of time needed to graduate.

15. In many cases, summer college courses can be taken at a less expensive school and the credits transferred to the full-time school. Students should check with their academic advisor, however, to be certain that any course taken at another school is transferable.

16. Most schools have placement offices that help students find employment, and all schools have personnel offices that hire students to work on campus. These employment programs are not based on financial need, and working is an excellent way to meet college expenses.

17. Most colleges and universities offer their employees a tuition reduction plan or tuition waiver program. Under this type of arrangement, the school employee and family members can attend classes at a reduced cost or no cost at all. This type of program is based not upon financial need, but rather on college employment.

18. Most colleges and universities sponsor resident advisor programs that offer financial assistance to students in the form of reduced tuition or reduced room and board costs in exchange for work in resident halls.

19. The Reserve Officers Training Corps (ROTC) Scholarship Program provides a monthly living stipend, as well as pays all tuition fees and textbook costs. Students should be certain, however, that they want this type of program before signing up because there is a service commitment after graduation.

20. Service Academy Scholarships are offered each year to qualified students to attend the U.S. Military Academy, the U.S. Air Force Academy, the U.S. Naval Academy, the U.S. Merchant Marine Academy, or the U.S. Coast Guard Academy. The scholarships are competitive and are based upon a number of factors, including high school grades, SAT or ACT scores, leadership qualities, and athletic ability. Students receive their under-graduate education at one of the service academies. They pay no tuition or fees, but there is a service commitment after graduation.

21. One of the most obvious ways of reducing college costs is to attend a low-cost school, either public or private. There are many colleges and universities with affordable tuition and generous financial assistance. Students should investigate all schools that meet their academic and financial needs.

22. Some schools offer combined degree programs or 3-year programs that allow students to take all of the courses needed for graduation in 3 years, instead of 4, thereby eliminat-ing 1 year's educational expenses.

23. Partial tuition remission for the children of alumni is a common practice. Parents and students should investigate their alma mater's tuition discount policy for graduates.

24. Some colleges and universities offer special discounts if more than one child from the same family is enrolled.

25. Some colleges and universities offer discounts to enrolled students if they recruit another student.

26. Some schools offer a tuition discount to student government leaders or to the editors of college newspapers or yearbooks.

27. Some colleges offer bargain tuition rates to older students.

28. Some colleges and universities convert non-federal school loans into non-federal grants if the student remains in school and graduates.

29. Some schools will pay a student's loan origination fees.

30. Some schools offer reduced tuition rates to families if the major wage earner is unemployed.

31. Some colleges and universities have special funds set aside for families who do not qualify for federal or state funding.

32. Some private colleges will match the tuition of out-of-state institutions for certain stu-dents. Check with your college to determine whether you qualify for this option.

33. Some companies offer tuition assistance to the children of employees. Parents and stu-dents should check with the personnel office for information.

34. Students should try to buy used textbooks.

Appendix

E

Students' Rights and Responsibilities in the College Admission Process

Reprinted with permission. Copyright 2009, National Association for College Admission Counseling.

Colleges Must Provide

General

- The cost of attending an institution, including tuition, books and supplies, housing, and related costs and fees
- Requirements and procedures for withdrawing from an institution, including refund policies
- Names of associations that accredit, approve, or license the institution
- Special facilities and services for disabled students

Academics

- The academic program of the institution, including degrees, programs of study, and facilities
- A list of faculty and other instruction personnel
- A report on completion or graduation rates at the college
- At schools that typically prepare students for transfer to a four-year college, such as community colleges, information about the transfer-out rate

Financial Aid

- The types of financial aid, including federal, state, and local government, need-based and non-need-based, and private scholarships and awards

- The methods by which a school determines eligibility for financial aid; how and when the aid is distributed

- Terms and conditions of campus employment, if financial aid is delivered through a work-study aid program

For more information about student financial aid, visit www.studentaid.gov.

Campus Security

- Procedures and policies for reporting crimes and emergencies on campus, as well as the system of adjudication

- The number and types of crime reported on and around campus

- The school's drug offense policy, as well as descriptions of the school's drug awareness and drug use prevention programs

To compare campus crime statistics for different colleges, visit http://ope.ed.gov/security.

Students' Rights in the College Admissions Process

Before You Apply

- You have the right to receive factual and comprehensive information from colleges and universities about their admission, financial costs, aid opportunities, practices and packaging policies, and housing policies. If you consider applying under an early admission plan, you have the right to complete information from the college about its process and policies.

- You have the right to be free from high-pressure sales tactics.

When You Are Offered Admission

- You have the right to wait until May 1 to respond to an offer of admission and/or financial aid.

- Colleges that request commitments to offers of admission and/or financial assistance prior to May 1 must clearly offer you the opportunity to request (in writing) an extension until May 1. They must grant you this extension and your request may not jeopardize your status for admission and/or financial aid.

- Some students choose to attend a community college for 1 or 2 years, and then transfer to a 4-year school. Tuition costs are substantially lower at community colleges than at 4-year institutions.

- Candidates admitted under early decision programs are a recognized exception to the May 1 deadline.

If You Are Placed on a Wait/Alternate List

- The letter that notifies you of that placement should provide a history that describes the number of students on the waitlist, the number offered admission, and the availability of financial aid and housing.

- Colleges may require neither a deposit nor a written commitment as a condition of remaining on a waitlist.

- Colleges are expected to notify you of the resolution of your waitlist status by August 1 at the latest.

Students' Responsibilities in the College Admissions Process

Before You Apply

- You have a responsibility to research and to understand and comply with the policies and procedures of each college or university regarding application fees, financial aid, scholarships, and housing. You should also be sure you understand the policies of each college or university regarding deposits you may be required to make before you enroll.

As You Apply

- You must complete all material required for application and submit your application on or before the published deadlines. You should be the sole author of your applications.

- You should seek the assistance of your high school counselor early and throughout the application period. Follow the process recommended by your high school for filing college applications.

- It is your responsibility to arrange, if appropriate, for visits to and/or interviews at colleges of your choice.

After You Receive Your Admission Decisions

- You must notify each college or university that accepts you whether you are accepting or rejecting its offer. You should make these notifications as soon as you have made a final decision as to the college you wish to attend, but no later than May 1. It is understood that May 1 will be the postmark date.

- You may confirm your intention to enroll and, if required, submit a deposit to only one college or university. The exception to this arises if you are put on a waitlist by a college or university and are later admitted to that institution. You may accept the offer and send a deposit. However, you must immediately notify a college or university at which you previously indicated your intention to enroll.

- If you are accepted under an early decision plan, you must promptly withdraw the applications submitted to other colleges and universities and make no additional applications. If you are an early decision candidate and are seeking financial aid, you need not withdraw other applications until you have received notification about financial aid.

Index

Notes

Notes

Notes

Get a plan to ace the exam—and make the most of the time you have left.

Whether you have two months, one month, or even just one week left, turn to the experts at CliffsNotes for trusted and achievable cram plans to ace the SAT and ACT exams—without ever breaking a sweat!

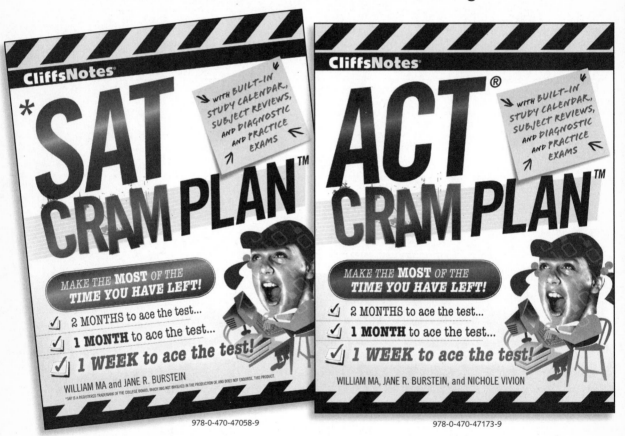

978-0-470-47058-9   978-0-470-47173-9

Each Cram Plan includes:

- **Diagnostic test** – helps you pinpoint your strengths and weaknesses so you can focus your review on the topics in which you need the most help
- **Subject reviews** – cover everything you can expect on the actual exam
- **Full-length practice test with answers and detailed explanations** – simulated SAT and ACT exams with scoring guides

For more study help, visit CliffsNotes.com
Available wherever books are sold.

CliffsNotes®
A Branded Imprint of ⓦ**WILEY**
Now you know.

*SAT is a registered trademark of the College Board, which was not involved in the production of, and does not endorse, this product.